Radicals and the
of the Churc

Lisa —

To add to your
puzzlements as
you switch tracks.

Mike.

Feb 90.

Don Cupitt

RADICALS AND THE FUTURE OF THE CHURCH

SCM PRESS LTD

British Library Cataloguing in Publication Data
Cupitt, Don
    Radicals and the future of the church.
    1. Theology
    I. Title
    230

    ISBN 0–334–02289–4

        First published 1989
          by SCM Press Ltd
26–30 Tottenham Road, London N1 4BZ

    Typeset at The Spartan Press Ltd
          Lymington, Hants
    and printed in Great Britain by
        Billing and Sons Ltd
            Worcester

If the foundations are destroyed,
What can the righteous do?

Psalm 11.3 (NEB)

For Ronald Pearse

Contents

Introduction   1

1 The Trouble with Believing   7

2 We are Grateful to Art   19

3 The Only Christianity that We Can Believe Now . . .   32
    (a) What has happened in philosophy   32
    (b) Sex, power and the production of reason   43
    (c) Religion after Truth   50
    (d) Theological fragments   56
    (e) Ethics and the imagination   62

4 . . . Is Unacceptable to the Church   70
    (a) Truth, power and social cohesion   70
    (b) Postmodernism and the question of God   79
    (c) Inequalities   89

5 Strategies for Christian Survival   100
    (a) Inside the church   100
    (b) Outside the church   116
    (c) Conclusion   123

6 What is to be Done?   127
    (a) Our Trojan horse   127
    (b) The discipline of the Void   135
    (c) Ethics after the end of history   145
    (d) The conquest of nihilism   158
    (e) Proposals   166

Notes   174

Index of Names   181

Introduction

On the small scale, this book addresses itself to the question of how far in the postmodern age a *church* is possible. A church surely requires at least some concentration of power, and some use of it to exert control over language, but if you are a thoroughgoing Christian heretic and dissident like me you cannot endure any attempt to control interpretation or finalize truth. The thing is impossible, anyway. In which case one should be like an uncommitted artist or a vagrant, and church membership seems to be a moral impossibility. In the monotheistic faiths the religious community has *always* been a power-structure and has *always* been in some measure coercive; so how can it change, at this time of day?

Considerations such as these may suggest that the future will belong to the post-ecclesiastical Christian poet, a type of which Kierkegaard was the first. Postmodernism is extremely 'minoritarian'. It loves small minorities, heretics, underdogs, outsiders and eccentrics, and is highly suspicious of all large concentrations of being, power and authority. I sympathize; but the political question cannot be bypassed. As we have come to recognize, it enters into one-to-one personal relationships and even into the constitution of the single individual. So as well as the small-scale question of how there can be a church, this book also broaches a larger question. Now that the historic basis of human association is breaking down, how can we rethink human community? In the sexual sphere, and *therefore* in the civic and religious realms also, the ancient politics of subjection is going to pass away. All human community hitherto has depended upon sexual subjection, and now we just cannot abide it any longer. I may be a man, but I can guess how women feel, because I myself simply cannot *bear* to be patronized or directed, or to be told what to feel, to do or to think, or to be confined within the straightjacket of other people's role-expectations. So I cannot regret the breakdown of all traditional structures of authority. I cannot accept them myself. But in that case we have a clear duty to ask what new basis for human social cohesion can be found.

Freud states the issues well, because he writes out of the heart of an ancient tradition of pure and uncompromising patriachal rule.[1] According to him the really important and primal human relationships that make society work are and must be highly unequal. There is always a ruler and those who are ruled, leader and led, star and fan, shepherd and sheep, master and man; and the led are bound to each other by and only by their common subjection to the leader. Two metaphors – but they are more than metaphors – make clear the nature of the leader's power. First, my response to my Lord and Master resembles the compulsive action of a hypnotized subject, and indeed every great leader with star quality is a kind of mesmerist. Secondly, 'the credulity of love is the most fundamental source of authority'. When we are in love we truly want to believe and to obey. Love is servitude.

So according to Freud human social cohesion is brought about first by the concentration of authority, secondly by its per-sonification, and thirdly by the erotic-hypnotic thraldom in which the leader holds the group. They really yearn to be led. From this account then it is clear that man is not 'a herd animal' but a 'horde animal, an individual creature in a horde led by a chief'. (In parenthesis, it is also clear that the church is the archetypal human community. Change it, and we'll change everything.)

Freud continues: If the leader is to become the unifying centre and focus of his followers' lives he must in himself be glorious, independent and self-sufficient while at the same time he requires of his followers the full surrender of their wills to his. He is invoked in a quasi-religious manner, his image is everywhere and he dwells in his followers' hearts. He becomes somewhat mystical and stylized. Oddly, the more godlike, exalted and uninvolved *he* gets to be, the more utterly prostrated and subjected to him his followers must get to be. The less he needs them, the more they need him. The greater his aseity the more profound their subjection, and the further this process is taken the more cohesive and powerful the group becomes. The more complete the collective inner subjection to the god, the more invincible the crusading army that results. Such is the true meaning of the slogan that man is a horde animal: communal and complete subjection to the will of the Father is the true key to power. The faithful prostrate themselves before him and are rewarded by being made able to lord it over everyone else. Hence the power of prayer.

In the later development of civilization the overwhelming violence and immediacy of the Father's domination is mitigated somewhat. He draws back a little, preferring now to exercise his rule indirectly through a Sacred Book, or through a corpus of Law which is interpreted and administered by a vast hierarchical organization. But behind the façade of an orderly bureaucratic process the ancient emotional tie to a dreaded-and-loved hypnotic persecuting Father still remains. The language his followers use, their body-postures, their rituals and the icons they treasure continue to be pervaded by the imagery of erotic subjection. Emotionally, the relationship of commoner to royalty, fan to star and follower to charismatic leader is the same as ever it was.

Now human societies naturally value most highly that which generates the greatest power and social cohesion, whether the power in question be sexual, military, religious or political. So the metaphysical tradition gives value-priority to that which is primal, unified, centred, selfsame, *a se*, unchanging, exalted, substantial, necessary and rational. Correspondingly, the religious tradition extols that which is lordly, mighty, exacting, holy, perfect, old, wise and all-controlling, and it commends those who are the most devoted, faithful and obedient. That is, the religious and metaphysical traditions commend those values and teach those myths that are going to make society strongest. Power comes first, and truth is for its sake. In a well-ordered universe everything is morally feminine in relation to what is above it in rank, and masculine in relation to what is below it in rank. Gender is relative: you look up attentive, deferential and quick to obey, and you look down with paternal cherishing supervision. But in every relationship someone must wear the trousers, as they used to say. It is ordained by God and Nature that man must rule woman, and the way that man knows, rules and possesses woman provides the fundamental model for every other case where *a subject is mastered*, whether we are talking of knowledge, of control in personal and social relationships, or of the use and enjoyment of property. Sexism is civilization.

Until as recently as Jacques Lacan – until, that is, only a generation ago – it could still be thought that this ancient patriarchal rationality, which had reached its most magnificent expression and development in Islam, was and would forever be constitutive of humanity, and compulsory. Human affairs just couldn't be conducted in any other way. Wrong. Lacan and those who think like him slip into the classic error of the dogmatic conservative sceptic by failing to grasp that their very articulation of their own position signs its death-warrant. Especially in these philosophy-of-life matters, a cultural situation is transformed when those subject to it become conscious of it. And in particular, as soon as the machinery by which patriarchical rationality is generated and operates had been described by Freud and Lacan, it began to pass away. They had thought that since (in their view) there was no alternative to it, it would survive their description of it. Not so. Described, it is transcended. We stand back from it, it is encapsulated, and it begins to recede into history. That is how our old Western culture died – through the invention of the very *concept* of culture, and by the way in which the hidden machinery of culture was exposed by Marx, Nietzsche and Freud. And that is why, although Freud was himself a conservative exponent of patriarchal rationality, he is still such a magnet for feminists. He liberates them, doing his work so well that he inadvertently overcomes himself.

All this, however, is water under the bridge by now. We are irreversibly committed to the search for a new order in human relationships, which means that we want to get sexual subjection out of the man-woman relationship, out of the public's relation to personalities in the world of mass communication, out of religion and out of politics. We want to escape from the traditional pyramid-structure of human organizations, and we want an end to the sadly alienated psychology that says that we are merely low life, ridiculous creatures by comparison with those who are the only real human beings, namely members of the royal family and a few other such stars.

From this it should be clear that I am not merely suggesting that feminism means trouble for God. Rather, I am suggesting that feminism is just one prominent facet of a more general revolt against patriarchal rationality, its structures of authority and its pyramidal rank-orders; and this is a revolt in which men are as active as women. The Green politics of Germany, post-structuralist theory in France, and the 'Alternative' culture of the Anglo-Saxon world are in their different ways all seeking a new kind of society in which the old hierarchies of domination, external authorities and concentrations of power have been replaced by a living horizontal network, a multicellular ferment of communication.

What might the church be and what might human relationships be in such a world, a world without domination, without timeless norms and fully post-historical? Let's ask.

This is the fourth and last of a series of books about faith in the postmodern age. *Life Lines* (1986) was about pathways in the religious life, *The Long-Legged Fly* (1987) was about language and the body, and *The New Christian Ethics* (1988) was about the quest for a plural and purely affirmative conception of the moral task. I hope that now that the series is complete their purpose and themes may be better understood.

Cambridge   D.C.

1

THE TROUBLE WITH BELIEVING

An important but neglected feature of the spiritual disorder of the times is that today there is sharp conflict between individual and group belief. For at least a century there have been people who think that the machinery by which groups of every sort generate and maintain their ideologies and their power is now sufficiently well-understood, and discredited, for it to be impossible any more for a reflective person to submit to any authority and accept its creed, or indeed to belong with a clear conscience to anything. One should live in the hills and walk in the free air, an alien and a wanderer, suspicious of all creeds and organizations and owing no allegiance to any of them. It's not that we trust ourselves, no, not at all, but that we actively distrust groups. Sooner or later they all of them become enemies of truth and freedom. We should stand apart, keep our own counsel, and come and go unannounced. In these times the only truth left to us is the truth of art, and art requires one to remain wholly uncommitted.

Not surprisingly, during the past hundred and fifty years similar tensions have appeared within the churches. The spoiled priest, the believer in a state of voluntary exile, the regretful fellow-traveller and the alienated theologian have become familiar characters. Quoting Kierkegaard, the classic example of this type, a senior American theologian recently described himself to me as 'one of Christianity's unhappy lovers'. For his own part this man has decided to remain silent and masked, taking the view that since his condition is quite incurable there is nothing whatever to be said or done about it. Others go public, forming a new kind of permanent internal opposition within the churches. In the nineteenth century the 'honest doubters' customarily left, and then tried to work out for themselves some sort of humanist or Spinozist substitute for the faith they had lost. But these substitutes were not much good, and in the present century many of us have chosen instead to stay, revisionist Christians within the church. We are like dissidents in an East European country: journalists from the outside world may sometimes seek us out, authority affects to disregard us, and our books circulate like *samizdat* publications.

We stay, even though we no longer think it very likely that the churches will reform and modernize themselves. It appears to be too late now. The churches seem to be planning to become slowly more rigid as they shrink. The people who might have had the strength and the courage to lead a modernization went some time ago, and only the most timorous are left. We stay, obstinately trying to keep a tradition alive, content just to survive and without very much expectation of success.

It may well be that the churches are correct in the decision they have made. Between, roughly, 1880 and 1960 it was quite widely believed that a critical orthodoxy was possible; that is, people thought that the new critical ways of thinking developed at the beginning of the nineteenth century could be fully assimilated by faith without transforming it too radically. A moderate and not-too-stressful reform would be sufficient to make the church intellectually and morally respectable again. People knew that there had been a crisis of faith; they dated it from the 1830s or so, and linked it with the names of Comte, Strauss, Feuerbach, Marx and Darwin. Tennyson's *In Memoriam* was a good introduction to it. But this crisis of faith, the one that our predecessors recognized, seemed to them to be manageable. The challenge that came from humanism and historical criticism of the Bible, from Marx, Darwin and Freud, could be met by a Christianity partly desupernaturalized, shorn of its crueller and more punitive doctrines, made more humane and recentred around the family, the neighbour, the eucharist and social action in this world. The crisis of faith was thus not terminal: it could be overcome.

The last great expression of this belief that the problem of faith in the modern world could be solved by a moderate church reform was the Second Vatican Council of 1962–1965, but it now seems to have come far too late in the day and to have been absurdly and hopelessly naïve. The churches may not understand much, but they have grasped the essential points, which are that the older reading of the nineteenth century was inadequate, that we are entering upon a much profounder world-cultural dissolution-and-transformation than used to be thought, and that acceptance of critical thinking must therefore eventually lead to conclusions far more radical than the churches can reasonably be expected to countenance. So, as all this became clear to them in the 1960s, the churches began to backpedal hard. They have largely disinvested in critical theology, and are instead taking up various forms of theological populism. Those who defend this move say just as it is authentically Christian to go down market morally, so it is also authentically Christian to go down market intellectually. As the Gospel is (especially) for sinners, so it is (especially) for decent, anti-intellectual folk.

Thus theological populism seeks to present itself as genuine 'conservative' Christianity; but the melancholy fact is that the more anti-intellectual the faith, the more vulnerable it is to politicization. The church's *defences* against modern thought are at the same time *gateways* for the entrance of modern politics. Knowing this, politicians invariably urge a simple populist faith upon the church. It will make her easier for them to control. And a populist Christianity that in effect serves the interests of the political Right becomes thereby just as much secularized as a church that has been taken over by the political Left, with the further disadvantage of also becoming philistine and morally vicious. In addition, during the past century the church's supernatural faith has by general consent been tacitly relegated to the cultural 'fringe'. The extent to which all this has already come about has marginalized those who still wish to maintain an older and more wide-ranging tradition of Christian thought, and has left us wondering if the phrase 'religious community' is not now becoming an oxymoron.

It seems that in the modern world the church is increasingly a vacuum, an empty shell which political forces rush to fill. In religion just as much as in politics, the Left and the Right move in and carve up the whole available space between themselves. Neither in Rome nor anywhere else, it seems, does any properly *religious* basis of association remain which is still vigorous enough to withstand the pervasive politicization of all life. But if it is the case now that no church can resist politicization, and that true religion (as Jesus is indeed reported to have taught) can be practised only in secrecy and solitude, then serious Christians should leave the church. They can try to do something for art and for writing, they can support the various human rights groups which attempt to defend individuals and minorities in the modern state, and above all they can and they must strive for the survival of religion. But they must do all these things on their own – or so it seems.

It is perhaps because the modern world has become so highly reflective that the ancient unconscious forms of religious solidarity have become enfeebled in our time. The problem now runs very deep. All our ancient religions are scriptural: like the rest of our culture, they are based on writing. In such a culture the exercise of public authority and the maintenance of truth-power depends in the last resort upon exegesis. The judge who interprets the law, the manager, the administrator, the examiner, the tester, the quality-controller, in a word the *official* who in every field maintains standards and supervises the way things are done, always goes by some form of rulebook. Society is based on the assumption that a competent and properly-trained official can possess the authority to interpret a text and apply it to a case in a way that can convince the public that he's got it right. Religion in particular says that there can be such a thing as a definitive interpretation, and there can be one who has the authority to state it. The Pope, for Catholics, is specially empowered definitively to interpret the church's teaching to the church's members. The Bible, for Protestants, is luminously self-interpreting or is luminously interpreted to the devout reader by God's Spirit within. In such ways we reveal our belief that authoritative interpretation is in principle possible. We can be told what's right: there can be a public Truth, held aloft like a standard.

In our Western group of cultures the doctrine of God has thus been foundational in that it functions to underwrite a whole series of socially necessary doctrines about language and its interpretation. God guarantees the ideas of absolute knowledge, complete control of meaning and final Truth, ideas that have provided the historic rationale for the exercise of public authority in the West. God is an almighty language-user, powerful enough to ensure that what *he* says doesn't get misunderstood and indeed cannot be misunderstood. God just is actual absolute mastery of meaning. He can make the Bible unambiguous, he can communicate timeless unchanging truths to us – and he can give exactly the backing that is needed to every sort of public official. Our entire culture has depended on the doctrines that a well-made text must have in the end just one definable, correct and masterable meaning, that God is the ultimate Master of all meaning, and that he can be relied upon to communicate something of his own mastery of meaning to the official, the scribe or interpreter who gives rulings in his name. Thus in Britain to this day sessions of Parliament and of the Courts still begin with prayer, and in oaths God is invoked to witness that what we are to hear is the truth whole and undistorted.

We see now what is meant by the idea of a defined and obligatory orthodoxy in the church. The church can have the right to tell me what to believe only insofar as meaning is masterable. But God *is* public authority, he *is* the Master of meaning, he *is* objective Truth. He ensures that his church gets the truth and thereafter remains infallibly or indefectibly in the truth. All the technical terms – inerrant, irreformable, infallible and so forth – amount in the end to the claim that a text can be conclusively interpreted. There is just one right meaning. The orthodox line when it has been duly laid down is clear, final and indisputable. It leaves no more to be said. It is public and objective truth and it has a right to bind my thinking.

However, over recent generations, and especially since the time of such pioneers as Mallarmé, C. S. Pierce and Nietzsche, we have simply lost all these basic doctrines about language, knowledge, meaning, truth and interpretation. Language now looks like an improvization, purely human, ever-changing, and bound into the human practices that it facilitates and furthers. Words do not share any qualities with the things out there in the world that they are used to refer to. Strictly speaking, words are related only to each other. There is no 'finalistic' or pre-established bond at all between language and reality. Reference is merely conventional. There is no Meaning out there and no Truth out there. Meaning and truth belong only within language, and language is only human, an historically-evolving and changing thing. Depending as it does only upon boundaries within language that are vague and shifting, meaning is no more than current usage. Meanings are not timeless essences. A meaning is like a footpath defined by an unspoken popular consensus, worn into its present course by many anonymous feet and in response to contingent practical needs, and therefore just a local, relative and changeable thing.

Further, since interpretations are always themselves open to further interpretation and meanings have to be described in terms of other meanings, and so on without end, meaning never gets to be absolute. The apocalyptic, finalizing disclosure of ultimate Truth is never reached. Both the *parousia* and the *arché*, the absolute End and the absolute Beginning, thus seem to be mythical notions. Neither is ever actually attained, simply because we are always within language, and language and interpretation are endless both ways. That is, there is no starting-point anywhere which is not already an interpretation and therefore questionable, and there can be no final interpretation which neither calls for nor permits any further comment. No absolute or fixed point is ever reached, either in the past or the future. Thus we see that critical thinking, questioning, arguments about interpretation and calls for further explanation are, *just in principle*, interminable both retrospectively and prospectively. We must quite forget all ideas of founding and final Truth. Like the universe of physics, the universe of philosophy is relativistic, finite, unbounded and outsideless.

This realization demythologizes language, knowledge, meaning, truth and interpretation. It demythologizes God and all public authority, and it ends the West not by closing it but by dispersing it into endlessness. Hear this: the West is over; hence the talk of postmodernism. Western culture was based on the idea of a Telos, a Goal of all life and final Truth that would be attained when science was completed, when the philosopher reached the Absolute, when the Parousia or the Kingdom of God arrived on earth, or when the soul stood before its Maker at the Last Judgment. This revelation of final Truth would vindicate all the steps that had led up to it, and all the lesser authorities who had appealed to it for support. But the astounding event that has come upon us in recent times is the end of all Ends. As in our modern physical cosmology, so also in our philosophy, everything now scatters into infinite dispersal and endlessness. We are adrift in an illimitable flux. Truth is a lot of arguments that go on forever, unsettled without end.

Yet this endless undecidability that follows the loss of the old absolutes is not all bad news. It opens a new space, and leads us to seek out a post-orthodox sort of Christian faith. Today, an individual's Christian faith is the outcome of a personal reading, interpretation and appropriation of text. By 'text' I mean everything that the Christian receives – and it is all made of signs. It is scripture and liturgy, doctrine and instruction, myth and symbol. This mighty flowing river of signs does not have just one true pre-established Meaning, out-there. It gets a meaning as it comes to life in me. I take it in, and its chains of interconnected signs enter my sensibility, evoking and channelling a play of feeling and so becoming interwoven with my life. I appropriate the text, make it mine and actualize it – and this is a creative activity, inevitably different in each person and different each time. But lest we should be thought to be reinstating individualism,[1] it might be better to say that the text actualizes a new meaning of itself every time it is read. Its authority lies not in its masterful control of just One Great Meaning but in its fecundity, its proliferation of meanings.

So we take, and cannot help but take, a thoroughly aesthetic and anarchistic view of meaning and truth. Aesthetic, in that the ascription of a meaning is inevitably and quite rightly an occasional and creative activity. We must make something of the text, or the text must make something of itself, as it interacts with the sensibility in which it is 'played' like a record or a tape. And we take an anarchistic view of meaning in that we deny that there is or can be any one final and over-ridingly authoritative interpretation. During the same period in which we have come to our modern view of text and interpretation the interpretative artist, the producer, director or conductor, has come to be regarded as a creative figure who is expected to produce a new reading of the score or the text. There isn't just one right Hamlet, and there is no way of limiting the range of possible future Hamlets waiting to be invented by directors and actors yet unborn. Each generation makes a new Hamlet and there is no last Hamlet. Just keep on inventing new Hamlets, will you? Similarly, any actualized or 'lively' Christian faith that we may be able to work out for ourselves must be and will rightly be one of our own invention. If you have not made it up, created it and put some new life of your own into it, then it can be no good to you. The only truly religious God is and has to be a man-made God. Your God has to be, let's be blunt about it, your own personal and temporary improvization. Our God is only able to be so close to us and to dwell in our hearts *because we made him*; that is, the word 'God' resounded in a distinctive way in us. We have no need to be apologetic or evasive about this, for the nature of Writing is such that it could not have been otherwise. 'God' (the word) comes to life in you as you read. Your faith just has to be your own personal creative interpretation of what you've been given. I am not going back to individualism, and I am not giving you any special credit for creativity. I am merely saying that this is how language is.

In this way the death of the old metaphysical God and the end of all absolute pre-established Meaning has cleared a space within which each believer is charged with the task of evolving her or his own personal meaning. What used to be called 'heresy' is now the standard requirement. Heresy and orthodoxy have changed places, in a way that has left us feeling acutely suspicious of every power-structure that still, anachronistically, tries to bring meaning under public and official control. Ideas of public rationality, objective truth, univocal meaning and orthodoxy are developed as tools of domination. They are monarchical ideas: one God, one Truth, one chain of command. But we argue for a dispersed God and a Pentecost-Christianity, and therefore for pure anarchy. The only true God is your own god, your personal god, the one who takes up his abode in your heart as a result of your own personal reading and appropriation of the Christian faith. The nature of writing is such that not even Shakespeare himself could have the power or the right to impose upon us, permanently, just one official, orthodox and authoritative reading of his works. Even if he had tried to do it, we would still fall to arguing about how to interpret his interpretation, for interpretation just is incurably plural and changeable; and even those who wish most determinedly to resist the implications of what I am saying cannot deny that the Holocaust has made *The Merchant of Venice* a different play, and that feminism has made *The Taming of the Shrew* a different play.

By the same token, I want to argue that the incurable plurality and endlessness of interpretation makes the very notion of a single publicly-established, authoritative, permanent and compulsory orthodoxy impossible either in society at large or in the church in particular. Truth cannot be determined once-for-all and objectively, but only evolved provisionally and *ad hoc*. Even if you disagree with me you must at least concede that any 'orthodox' interpretative settlement arrived at may itself give rise to disputes about how to interpret it or may suddenly find itself overthrown and made obsolete by historical change, from which it follows that no orthodoxy can hope to be timeless and history-proof. But if you *agree* with me that in our culture, based as it is on Writing, the incorrigible plurality, endlessness and disputability of interpretation make it altogether impossible officially to control meaning and truth, then for us every orthodoxy is already relativized. The traditional rationale for the exercise of public authority has broken down, leaving us with a clear choice between tyranny and anarchy.

By 'tyranny' I mean non-rational, authoritarian and populist modes of operation in church and state. The leadership guides, manipulates and exploits popular feeling. By 'anarchy' I mean the thoroughgoing repudiation of any unitary control or closure of interpretation, and the acceptance instead of a genuinely open and limitlessly heretical and mobile social and religious order. 'Anarchy' is truth proliferating unchecked by any supreme standard or disciplinary control. We all appreciate the need for anarchy in art. Paul Feyerabend has well argued the case for it in science.[2] *De facto*, we already have it in religion, morality and politics, where we all know that the arguments are endless. So our only problem is to admit and to see the implications of what we are already perfectly well aware is the case. Meaning and truth are like mushrooms; they have to keep springing up afresh all over the place. Religion and morality are like art: we make them up, they are indefinitely variable, finality or closure is never reached, and all public and compulsory orthodoxies are dead. Sometimes there is a need to work for a local public consensus and to get it written into public rules; but any such consensus was made by us, gets it authority from us and is subject to revision by us. We must admit our responsibility for what we ourselves have made. And insofar as the older, mainline churches nevertheless remain unable to acknowledge all this, and cling to their cherished orthodoxies and dreams of spiritual power, they must provoke the dissent from which we began.

The trouble with believing today, then, is that the churches persist and our own psychology persists in clinging to ideas of fixed meaning, authoritative interpretation, orthodoxy and final Truth. In an age when language has become completely enhistorized and humanized these ideas are no longer tenable, but we hold on to them because of our obsession with power, our desire to be governed and our reluctance to grow up.

In 1977 Penguin Books published a book by J. L. Mackie called *Ethics: Inventing Right and Wrong*. The subtitle makes the message of the book perfectly clear, and yet the publisher chose to issue it with the full title printed on the cover over a picture of a colossal Hand from Above pointing a little blue-suited Everyman down a single ready-made straight and narrow path! The absurd contradiction between the printed book-title and the front-cover picture is also a contradiction within all of us between the head and the heart, the believer and the church, the conscious and the unconscious. The old systems of repression are still alive in our hearts and therefore in our institutions. They are part of what Deleuze is teaching us to think of as the social unconscious.[3] It is old and ugly, but it remains obstinately alive.

Historically a 'free' church has so far meant a church which has enjoyed the fullest liberty to bully its own members without outside interference. The notion that *internal* doctrinal pluralism within the church is positively a good thing has been rare, and enjoyment of *moral* pluralism has been rarer still. But a really free church will be a church whose power-structure has decayed because people no longer find difference offensive to them.[4] Such a church will rejoice in being highly pluralistic, a tapestry of diverse Christianities all adding up to an aesthetically beautiful, morally-variegated and ever-changing whole. Why *shouldn't* the faith mean something different to each Christian? Realism in philosophy, religion and morality is produced by an unconscious yearning to be ruled and told what is right and good for us. We are hooked on that image of a Mighty Hand pointing out the right path, guiding, protecting and delivering us all alike. But when we give up that unconscious yearning to be dominated *all alike*, we will find that we no longer need the mutual recriminations, the factionalism, the moral bullying, the objective God and the power-structure. That will clear the field, and give us the duty and the courage to develop each of us his and her own personal faith. We won't need a common authority when we no longer need to be all alike.

The church as it is is rather different. Almost from the very beginning it has been a punitive power-structure with an orthodoxy. It has worked by taking our god out of our heart, objectifying him and universalizing him. It then enthrones him as Lord over us all alike. He is thus used as a *symbol* of the church's power over the believer, he is used to *legitimate* the church's power and, most important of all, he is used as a *front*. By hiding behind him the church is able to work unceasingly and almost unnoticed to extend its power over the souls of believers. Thus Christians are usually quite unaware that what they think of as the worship of God is often rather their own systematic dechristianization. The work of Christ was to transfer divinity from Heaven to the heart. In Christ the old objectified power-God was humanized, broken up, dispersed and poured out as Spirit into each human heart, to be known under a different name in each. So the objective God-out-there was turned into a personal and subjective god-within. But much of our supposedly Christian worship sets out to reverse the movement. It takes the personal god out of our hearts, projecting and consolidating him so that he becomes the Monarch of the community, which he then rules through the hierarchy, who have the franchise on his authority, power and truth. As a result, to this day our value-judgments tend to favour unity, selfsameness, agreement, discipline, order, leadership and patriarchal control. The church's task is to assist the government on the moral front by turning people into sheep because, as we all know, sheep are emblems of Christian virtue.

Our present argument, however, has tended in the opposite direction. The major faiths are scriptural, both in the narrow sense of being ostensibly based on sacred books, and also in a broader sense in that they are mediated to us in very large bodies of language-like material: symbols, forms of life and rituals, as well as writings and forms of words. Each knows from its own history that it has always been subject to divergent interpretations. Today, in the age of the interpretative artist, in the age

when language has come down to earth and become fully
enhistorized, in the age when we see that interpretation is
omnipresent, endless, and endlessly plural, why may not a
hundred flowers bloom?

2

WE ARE GRATEFUL TO ART

Talk of overcoming orthodoxy and letting a hundred flowers bloom is all very well, but the West has had very little experience of thoroughgoing pluralism in philosophy, morality and religion. Even yet, most of us remain committed to our traditional One-God-one-Truth-one-Self metaphysics. To become a real pluralist you must (among other things) give up the spiritual-substance view of the self and instead see yourself as just a collection of roles, faces and functions. You have to see yourself as being all on the surface, the sum of your own external relations. Not easy, for most of us. A real pluralist, able to say with Durkheim and in his sense that 'all religions are true', and yet also truly committed and practising, was scarcely possible before Nietzsche. At least, such a person was scarcely possible among philosophers and theologians, because they thought their trade committed them to privileging systematic unity and self-consistency. Among artists and literary people, who are in many cases by nature masked, evasive and plural, the situation was rather different, as we shall see. Otherwise the chief forerunners of our presently-emerging ultra-pluralism were syncretism, scepticism and relativism, but none of these went as far as we now have to go. The syncretist did not renounce the dream of One Truth, but merely reinstated it at a higher level. Like Vivekananda, or like John Hick in our own time, he would claim that the same God (or Absolute, or mystical state) is known by different names in different parts of the world, and that the various major religions are simply so many different pathways all leading ultimately to the same Goal. But this only shows us that *intellectually* syncretism has not advanced one step beyond Western Philosophy, or beyond traditional Christianity and Islam. The ancient privileging of systematic unity, self-consistency and Presence, although transposed from the usual one-faith level to a multi-faith level, is otherwise retained unquestioned. But today the task is not to give these old deep assumptions a new lease of life by promoting them to a global and multi-cultural level, but rather to expose and criticize them. Why, for example, do we *want* One Truth? Why not instead create many truths, like an artist?

The sceptic in the style of Montaigne, who was often also a relativist and a fideist, might seem to be our ancestor in a more nearly direct line. He repudiated capital-T Truth, having observed that gods, customs, moralities and ways of constructing the world are different at different places and times, and he therefore practised the local religion because there was no compelling capital-R Reason not to do so. It makes sense – and is prudent – to join in the local festivals and other customs. But this person was passive and quietistic, living before Kant and Hegel and the philosophy of art. (The greatest of modern achievements – *the invention of invention*.) The sceptic thought the way to salvation was consciously to withhold assent and to remain in tranquil belieflessness. He did not think of saying that fulfilment is to be found in the creative affirmation, the proliferation and indeed the active production of many truths. But that is what we want to say today.

This relatively new position, thoroughgoing and postmodern pluralism, is sometimes called 'aestheticism'. It begins with the Romantics, with whom the philosophy of art first became central to the understanding both of religion and of philosophy generally. However, the earlier Romantics usually still sought an ultimate systematic unity in Hegel's manner, and tended to give priority to the aesthetic contemplation of nature and works of art; and these two features of their work made it look at first as if they were merely continuing, albeit perhaps somewhat modifying, the old platonic tradition which had always seen the Goal of life as the contemplation of the One, the Real, the Good, the True and the Beautiful.[1] Only with Nietzsche does the message come through really loud and clear that primacy is to be given *not* to contemplation and Unity, but to creativity and plurality. We are grateful to art, he says, for leading the way and showing us that we do not need a Cosmos or objective Truth, nor any ultimate unity and finality. We can quite well build our own house to live in out of the materials available.

So art finds no reason to complain that reality offers us nothing but fleeting loose ends, fictions and contingencies. That'll do well enough. What more do we need? After all, if it had actually been the case that every aspect of reality could be integrated and totalized into a systematic unity, in the manner portrayed in the philosophies of Spinoza or Leibniz, then the world itself would be the one and only absolute work of art and there would be nothing left for human art to do but admire it and perhaps make little celebratory copies or models of it. But art is needed (as faith is needed) precisely because the world is *not* a perfect and ready-made cosmos. Indeed, it is because we all know this that there is tragedy. And so Nietzsche further threatens the end of philosophy by attacking its beginning and saying that the coming of Socrates was a disaster, for it spelt the death of tragedy. The older sacred tragic drama had been superior to Philosophy both in the way it had represented to us our human condition, and in the remedy it provided. A Christian might rather similarly say that to stand alongside the afflicted, to experience evil and also perhaps just to take part in the Good Friday Liturgy, is better than to read or to write yet another vain book about 'the Problem of Evil'.

Put it another way: which gives the better, the more productive, the profounder representation of the human condition, and which tells us more about ourselves and our life – the corpus of Leibniz or that of Shakespeare? Leibniz is as committed an exponent as any of the classic Philosophical values of the West, exalting absolute knowledge of the Necessary, a knowledge that is timeless, immediate, complete, *a priori*, systematic, apodictic and dogmatic. In the enjoyment of such knowledge consisted our beatitude. Being there to be its object, God guaranteed that such knowledge was attainable; and such knowledge, being attainable, must have God there to be its object. Thus God and absolute knowledge were yoked together, and indeed realistic or metaphysical theism affirmed in the strongest possible terms the grounding and unification of every aspect of reality in one infinite Spirit, and thereby also the grounding, the fulfilment and the ultimate totalization of every scrap and facet and particle of our knowledge into one absolute intellectual vision.

Remarkable: but the public have decided in favour of Shakespeare, whose corpus is radically plural and must be experienced and studied as art. If they now get more out of Shakespeare than out of Leibniz are we not to conclude that the public have decided they don't want absolute knowledge any longer? If Leibniz were right, a systematic philosophical presentation of whatever it is that Shakespeare is supposed to have to say to us would be more worth having than what he actually wrote. But nobody thinks that, so nobody thinks that Leibniz is right. In which case it would appear that Nietzsche has been vindicated and that we are indeed all aestheticists nowadays. We have decided that the Meaning of It All is something indefinitely plural that is endlessly made and remade, celebrated and lamented *by us* in art, and not something absolutely single, selfsame, intelligible and timeless that can be known by pure rational intuition. And if it is thus true that the artistic vision is deeper and more powerful than that of Philosophy, why may not religious thought in the future make the same kind of alliance with art as it has hitherto had with Philosophy? Why should not religion become spontaneously plural and creative?

Just at present we are in a curious intermediate situation. The culture as a whole has gone aestheticist, indeed very obviously so, while yet the typical doctrines of aestheticism or Nietzscheanism still provoke great indignation amongst many philosophers and theologians. No wonder the public have largely given up philosophy and theology as no longer interesting subjects. But just as the philosophers find it hard to get away from the logocentric values of traditional capital-P Philosophy, so the religious find it virtually impossible to imagine Christian faith without orthodoxy, censoriousness, repression and factionalism – without, in a word, the whole apparatus of a 'regime of truth'. Derrida has shown in detail how all of Philosophy's founding distinctions involve a 'violent hierarchy'.[2] Every time something gets privileged something else gets put down, devalorized and repressed. Acts of violence created Reason and made Philosophy possible.

The same is true of religion: without even needing to think about it we all instinctively and rightly associate the strongest forms of Christianity, the strongest faith and the strongest church, with confessional unanimity based on a monistic view of religious truth, with zeal and firmness of conviction and purpose, and with strict discipline and control. Religious strength equals firmness of repression. Western philosophy has always privileged form, unity, reason, consciousness, self-sameness, substance – that is, lucid authoritative patriarchal control, which views the subjection of woman as the model for all other forms of order, mastery, possession and knowledge. Western theology correspondingly affirms One God, one Lord, and *therefore* one principle of authority and chain of command; one Truth, one Faith and one Church to teach it, and *therefore* within the church an orderly many-tiered pyramidal hierarchy who are Truth's spokesmen. These ideas are strong, really strong, so strong indeed that the obvious retort to our argument so far is that there have already been plenty of weak churches, creedless denominations, liberal Christian groups without a strong power-structure – and where are they now? They are not doing very well. The forms of Christianity that survive longest and have the highest prestige are the least liberal and the most authoritarian, grand, spectacular and cruel. People want cruelty, they know that cruelty is strength, and they admire cruel religion. Cruelty endures; cruelty is truth. For the fact is that every cultural institution and tradition that is going to bite deep and last long – be it science, religion, philosophy, morality, art or whatever – can become established only by some measure of pain and violence and discipline. If there is to be any group then it must impose a measure of penal discipline upon its members, and if you don't like that then you may as well not bother to have the group. Similarly, if there is to be any pursuit of individual excellence then there has to be an ascetical self-discipline whose imposition will deform the personality and cause pain.

So the difficulty in what we have been saying about a pluralistic, free and creative sort of church is clear. How can it be strong, and how can it endure? We want a community, but we baulk at the price of membership. We vainly suppose that there could be a genuinely liberal and plural community, a community without pain and without pressure in which truth would flow freely without being harnessed by power – as if you could somehow *separate* truth, community and power from each other. Which is naïve. We are like tourists watching a village procession on a saint's day in Sicily. We admire folk religion. We wish we still had something like that in our own lives. Where did we go wrong? In religious ritual people are able communally and symbolically to affirm their sense of the solemnity, the sweetness, the brevity, the seriousness, the terror and the joy of our life. That is good. Couldn't we all just take part *at that level*, setting aside the power-structure, the psychological cruelty and the superstitious beliefs of traditional religion? Sorry, no. If you want to take part in that peasant procession and have the tragic solemnity, the holiness and the brief joy of life affirmed in you, by you and for you by the community acting through you, then you must pay the necessary price. You can only have that solemn joy laid on for you, given to you, by subjecting yourself unreservedly to an ancient and harsh communal regime of truth. The tourist supposes it can be had on the cheap, and it can't. You cannot have the consolations of religion expressed in and through you by the power of the community without subjecting yourself to that power. By your subjection you purchase the values.

So the anti-intellectual and authoritarian Catholicism typified by, for example, Evelyn Waugh is in its own way more logical and more rational than our pluralistic liberal theology. If you want the communal solidarity and the communal affirmation of precious values, then you had better accept the supernatural beliefs, the repression, the cruelty and the authoritarianism. It is all one package. Alternatively, if you want to go over to an art-model then you must do all the toilsome creative work yourself. You may, for example, follow Joseph Beuys in working out a private mythology, being an enchanter rediscovering dark-age and even shamanistic values, trying to remake Western culture after its end – and doing it by strenuous labour, as an artist and alone. If you want your religious meaning provided for you by the community then you must put yourself in the community's power. Alternatively, you can make it for yourself as an artist would; but that too is costly, though in a different way.

This shows how we differ from Bernard Williams. Williams says in effect that the religious consciousness as such is obsolete and cannot now be recovered. He rather likes Christianity, and certainly while in Cambridge would occasionally attend his College Chapel and read the lesson. His general orientation in morality, politics and culture is, at least in a background sense, Christian. But for him there is no way back, for an impassable gulf separates him from actual membership of the church. One of his ways of summarizing the argument is as follows: religion begins with a picture of the world as being run by God pretty much as a heavy father might run his family or a king might rule his kingdom. God issues moral commandments, backing them with promised rewards and threatened punishments. These sanctions are not in themselves absurd. On the contrary, they make a lot of sense, for if the religious account is true and the world is indeed run like that, then the sanctions give us excellent reasons for acting justly and respecting other people's interests. Unfortunately though, the simple religious picture of how the world is run *cannot* be true, 'since if we understand anything about the world at all, we understand that it is not run like this'.[3] So the ethical consciousness is compelled to move on and seek a new rationale for morality. 'But then', says Williams, 'if ethical understanding is going to develop, and if religion is going to understand its own development in relation to that, it seems inevitable that it must come to understand itself as a human construction; if it does, it must in the end collapse.'

Williams' argument is that the very activity of the liberal or revisionist theologian, as he busily reformulates religious belief in response to changed cultural conditions, must eventually destroy religion. The better he does his job, the more he inadvertently demythologizes religion by exposing it as being just man-made. By rewriting the doctrine of God in response to feminism we admit it was man-made in the first place. And this, Williams thinks, brings the religious consciousness to an end. There's no escaping Williams' conclusion – if it is indeed the case that religion cannot survive the realization that it is a human construction.

I differ from Williams at just this point. I say you can still be religious after you have recognized that religion is only human. Especially in the Americas, feminist theologians, political theologians and black theologians are rewriting God and bending him into all manner of new shapes without, it seems, writing themselves out of religion. I have chosen to emphasize especially the case of religious art because nobody can deny, first that works of art are just human constructions, secondly, that great religious art, such as the late paintings of Mark Rothko, can still be produced, and thirdly, that such works as Rothko's can be quite new and independent of existing religious groups, their teachings and iconographies. I want to say that Rothko (for example: he is by no means the only one) just invented works of art that are great religion. Indeed, I maintain that the major artists of Modernism and after – roughly, since the mid-1860s – can be viewed as the prophets of a new religious order. From their dedication to their task, their creativity and their works many people now get the sort of charge that earlier generations once got from icons and the cult of saints.

So there seems to be no difficulty in the thought that there can be great religion that knows it is just man-made. For there is undoubtedly great religious art which is non-cognitive or non-realistic, which borrows nothing from any extant tradition and which makes no metaphysical or supernatural claims. It is pure invention. So for me the problem is not the same as it is for Bernard Williams. He thinks the religious consciousness as such is obsolete because it has become obvious that religion is a human construction. But I say that you can *easily* go on being religious and creating religion in the full awareness that religion is only human. I do it. And since Christianity was always profoundly humanistic and Buddhism has never actually needed any super-natural beliefs, these two faiths in particular should in principle be able to adapt themselves to the new situation. But I am seriously concerned about whether a church is still possible. For the modern sort of art-religion that I have been describing is highly charismatic. That is, it is produced by specially-gifted individuals, it erupts suddenly and ceases equally suddenly, and it cannot be institutionalized, routinized or produced to order. Painting in particular is super-charismatic, in that it was the first of the arts to begin living after the end of its own history in that queer post-modern condition in which it has to operate by continually reinventing itself. We don't get anywhere. There is no Telos. We joyfully celebrate a pure magical creativity that creates even itself. We keep restarting. The establishment of a settled tradition is impossible, and although dozens or perhaps hundreds of little groups are formed, each of which solemnly issues its manifesto, they can stick together and work in a common style for only two years, or five years, or so.

Such is the post-modernity of painting: the religious parallel to it is the proliferation of small transient religious sects and the increasing extent to which everyone now feels charged with the task of working out her own path through life, view of life and task in life. Enduring communal religion in the past worked by a system of unconscious coercion. Today that doesn't seem to work any more. People just hate being got at at that unconscious level. Even we professionals who have perhaps been priests for decades, who theoretically cordially *approve* of all our rituals and are thoroughly habituated to them – even we may still find it acutely embarrassing and difficult to dress up, to play a part and enact a ritual. In some way we are too reflective or self-conscious to function easily in the mode or at the level at which religious groups have traditionally operated. We do not like being pressurized, got at or influenced at that level, nor do we find it easy to get at or communicate with other people at that level. We have become – too prickly, is it?

We are no longer social beings in the way we once were. Extraordinary. Are you with me? We have lost our trust in a certain deep unconscious communality at the level where the individual used to be united with the group, the level at which communal beliefs, communal symbols, communal patterns of performative ritual action used to be generated and participated in. For a lot of people all this doubtless still works, but for many of us it just doesn't and can't any more, so that we are no longer suitable material for the old type of church. And we cannot do a thing about it.

Now we see how tough the problem of church renewal is. It certainly is not a matter of writing a new orthodoxy, but nor is it just a matter of abolishing all creeds and tests of faith, loosening things up and becoming much more relaxed, tolerant, open and pluralistic. We seem to need a quite new kind and a quite new mechanism of religious association – if, that is, we need a church at all.

Do we? After all, it is nearly one-and-a-half millennia since Justinian shut down the Academy, yet platonism has managed to continue as a living cultural force. It has lived on within other institutions religious and educational, and as a literary tradition. If platonism can get on in this way without its own distinct institutional embodiment, why may not Christianity do so too? Some think this is already happening. They may see religion as having already been transformed into Writing, or into art; and there are others who point out how most religious people and much of religious thought are already outside the church. Even at the simplest level the number of people who think of themselves as Christian, claim to pray and so forth, is several times the number of those who still regularly attend church.

Some have gone on from this to argue for forcibly imposed and radical church reform. Recent attempts to abolish the church in Eastern Europe have a history going back to the French Revolution, and indeed the early nineteenth century saw more serious consideration of the possibility of drastically reforming the church than there has been at any other epoch in modern history. France experimented with secular religions, Prussia was in the era dominated by Hegel and Schleiermacher, and even England had her Thomas Arnold.[4] In all three countries there were those who saw clearly the connections between supernatural belief, repression, clerical privilege, and indifference to the poor. And at that time almost everyone wished to undo the church as the obstructive, separatist and arrogant institution it has characteristically been. As the lineal but universalized descendant of the synagogue, the church has always been a mass movement and a highly organized and self-conscious society, a sort of nation in exile or spiritual Empire, a ghostly counterpart of the state within the state but making grander claims for itself, to the state's intense irritation. The church further annoys the state by having its own system of government, hierarchy, courts, discipline, ideology, culture, ethic and strong instinct for survival and for power. It is a powerful enemy, on which the state often wishes to take revenge.

However, unlike our predecessors of the early nineteenth century, we today find ourselves unexpectedly warming to this catalogue of the church's charms. It suddenly occurs to us that all this is too good to lose, and in any case cannot be wished away either by the state or by commentators. It is too good to lose, because so detestable and threatening is the modern state over most of the world that we urgently need to support anything tough enough to stand up to it. People do not need to be told how useful it is to have the church as a focus of dissent, a rival power-centre and a defender of human rights. It is a good opposition, a conspicuous flag for protesters to rally to. So in spite of its still-lingering repressiveness, its disastrous weaknesses on the doctrinal front and its very heavy loss of membership, the church may well be under less direct political threat to its existence now than it was in 1820. On the whole it is more popular now than it was then.

The priorities in church reform are therefore rather different today from what they were in the generation or so after the French Revolution. With the usual exceptions, the church does not just now look excessively cruel or corrupt, and the clergy do not look as if they are wedded to an *ancien régime* that is about to be swept away. On the ethical-political front we would in general like the church to be more pushy, aggressive and confident than it is. Alas, the problem is that the church has historically drawn all her confidence in herself, her mission, her distinct identity and her moral authority from a certain set of supernatural beliefs – and these beliefs are dead. Even those who still say they hold them cannot actually *do* anything effective with them any longer, because they do not connect and mesh in with the public world we presently inhabit. Add to this the other considerations which we have advanced, considerations which as I claim have utterly demythologized and scattered all our historic ideas about institutional power and authority, orthodoxy and strength, and we see how severe our present situation is. Ethically at least, we need a church. It alone can give publicity and stability to our religious vocabulary. It is a theatre in which we solemnly enact our deepest feelings about the human condition. It guards and it also develops our moral tradition, pioneering new values and acting as an experimental nursery of new lifestyles. And it is a mighty fortress, a defence against the modern state. All this we need; but can a church that now knows it's only human, a church that is willy-nilly pluralist, creative and tolerant, hope to maintain sufficient unity and moral confidence for its ethical task? How can the church be *strong* without the supernatural legitimation and the mechanisms of repression from which it drew its former strength?

Struggling to keep up her confidence, the church just at present clings all the more desperately to the supernatural beliefs that in the past gave her legitimacy and nourishment. But the beliefs are hopelessly vague. They have lost meaning and efficacy. There is no help in them, and the very anxiety with which she clutches at them actually accelerates the church's slide into a closed cult mentality. The beliefs don't pump the church up any more, so instead she has to pump *them* up. Faith in them has to become more authoritarian and fideistic. They become like compulsory formulae or passwords, shibboleths imposed by the church on her members. She comes down like a ton of bricks on anyone who dares to point out how hollow and blurred they have become. But this is a wretched situation. The church becomes increasingly the prisoner of her own wilfully-maintained state of self-deception, and people of goodwill are forced out because she is no longer able to grant them sufficient spiritual space in which to live a tolerably honest, clear-headed and truthful religious life.

For many years now, I – and others – have been urging the church to get rid of all, and I mean *all*, of her supernatural beliefs. The present discussion has suggested that I need to answer one or two questions. The first group of questions are long-term, and concern the church. Suppose that Christianity were to become fully demythologized and expressed in purely human terms; suppose that the church indeed gave up all her supernatural beliefs: could she still remain the church? Without her old supernatural backing could she have the confidence to be an innovator, a force for change and a chronic headache for the politicians? For three millennia, since Samuel and Nathan, religious leaders have had in principle a certain moral leverage over the government because it has been believed or half-believed that they spoke a word from God. The ability of the bishops to give the politicians a fright has depended upon the notion that somehow the bishops have a more direct line to a higher moral Authority than any civil ruler can claim. What is to replace that notion?

This is not a small matter. It is important in itself and important also because it is connected with a number of other questions, all concerned with how after supernaturalism we are to envisage the church's morale, her authority, her identity, her sense of destiny and her grip on her membership. Hegel and others of his generation thought that once you had given up the old two-worlds cosmology (the world below and the world above, nature and grace, flesh and spirit), there could no longer be any reason to have two distinct societies, the state and the church. Blending them together, he sacralized the state and opened the way to the political messianism and the totalitarianism of later generations. Whether or not he himself is to be blamed for it, that bitter history has made us wary of Hegel's method of mediation by which everything is reconciled and synthesized into a higher unity. If everything, but *everything*, gets taken up into the Whole then no external standpoint is left from which any deep disagreement, criticism or protest can be voiced. Just for the sake of freedom therefore, we need to have plurality and value-conflict, and we warm to the idea of the church as a distinct society older and greater than the state, with her own values and her own critical and prophetic task. It is an idea that deserves to be salvaged, if possible.

That brings us to the second little cluster of questions. Our discussion so far has been merely theoretical. Reform is not in sight. The church appears locked into long-term decline, growing rigidity and a slide into fantasy and the cult mentality. So what is the individual to do in the meanwhile? Can we stay in the church, hidden, camouflaged and biding our time? Shall we accept the marginalization that they thrust upon us and become fellow-travellers, on the fringe? Ought we to be vociferous dissidents, perhaps organized, or would we do better to leave and begin work on something whose general shape we can already descry, namely the next stage in the history of religion?

This last question is particularly poignant. If our general argument points to an outlook which is anti-realist, highly pluralistic and world-affirming, post-historical and aestheticist, then why are we still so attached to the church, which is in every respect just the opposite of all this?

3

THE ONLY CHRISTIANITY THAT WE CAN BELIEVE NOW...

(a) What has happened in philosophy

Around Easter 1988 internal mail in Britain was being post-marked with the slogan 'JESUS IS ALIVE' and a cross. As might be guessed, an Evangelical businessman had paid the Post Office a large sum for this to be done, and he thereby sparked off a good deal of public controversy. Some commentators found instantly in favour of the slogan, whereas others after due and weighty consideration declared that in their view the evidence for it was insufficient. A third group were chiefly concerned to make the point that the slogan could appear intrusive and offensive. You got it stamped on your mail whether you liked it or not, and Rabbi Julia Neuberger for one did not like it.

So unphilosophical a country is Britain that even writers hate to pause long enough to think about language, and not a single person raised the question of what exactly it might *mean* to say that Jesus is alive. They all seemed confident that they just knew what it means and all that remained was for them to pronounce on whether it was true or not, and whether it was bad manners to have it stamped on people's mail without their consent.

Yet just what it means to say that Jesus is alive is in fact far from clear. The people who pay out retirement pensions have their own criteria for establishing whether a particular pensioner is still alive or not, but nobody thinks criteria of this type are applicable to the case of Jesus. Doctors have criteria for determining whether a badly-injured or terminally-ill patient is still alive or not, but again these criteria do not fit the case of Jesus. We do not set out to search for Jesus in the same way as we might search for a missing person. In fact he doesn't seem to satisfy *any* of the ordinary criteria for being alive as you are alive. They don't seem to be appropriate. So it seems that he must be alive in the metaphorical sense invoked when people say that some dead but still charismatic pop star or political figure 'lives'. Thus people say of Elvis Presley that 'the King lives', as they have also been known to say that John Lennon lives, that Che lives and that Haile Selassie lives. What is meant in a case like this is that we are still as much under the dead person's spell as ever, we are keeping his memory green, we venerate him, we cherish what he stood for and won't let it die, and so on. This usage clearly fits the case of Jesus far better. It seems then that 'Jesus is alive' doesn't make any factual claim, because the criteria for listing someone as factually still alive that are used by pension funds and doctors are obviously wholly inappropriate. Anyway, people don't live in that plain biological sense for 1990-odd years. 'Jesus is alive' has surely therefore got to be a fan's declaration of allegiance. Like 'Long live the King!', it expresses something rather than asserts something.

Thus if you take the common English view of language and regard the predicate 'is alive' as having first a straightforward literal or factual sense, and secondly an extended or metaphorical sense, then in your philosophy of religion you must quickly reach the conclusion that religious assertions are not factual. They are expressive declarations of loyalty and commitment.

Two things, however, are wrong with this view. The first is that it enrages the orthodox, who regard it as a monstrously inadequate and reductionist interpretation of what they mean. The second is that it does not explain why Rabbi Julia Neuberger takes such offence. Why should a purely personal declaration of allegiance cause her discomfort? She would after all be unlikely to take offence if she heard a Frenchman cry 'Vive la France!', or a teenager exclaim 'John Lennon lives!' We all know that tastes and allegiances differ, and the mere fact that somebody else's loyalties are not identical with my own is not by itself enough to justify a complaint.

The obvious response to all this is to point out that someone who says that Jesus is alive believes him to be truly alive but not with an ordinary biological life, for Jesus is alive beyond death or on the far side of death; and this is held to be a second *but also factual* sense of 'is alive'. It may be compared with the kind of life attributed to gods and spirits: they too are thought to 'live', but in a supernatural and non-biological way. It has to be admitted that we have no direct experience or understanding of this second way of being alive, but lots of people believe in life after death. Indeed, believers in life after death are so numerous that it would surely be absurd to claim that they don't know what they mean by it. And if people know what they mean by life after death for the righteous in general, then they must surely know what they mean by claiming that Jesus lives. He lives like all others of the righteous dead.

So now Jesus is being thought of as alive in some mysterious and other-worldly sense that cannot be fully spelled out in this-worldly terms but which must be presumed to be clear enough, even if not wholly clear, to religious people themselves.

Yet there is still a difficulty: many Jews and most Rabbis surely believe in a blessed life after death for the righteous, and accept nowadays that Jesus the teacher of Nazareth was one of the righteous men of Jewish history. It seems to follow that he lives as do other martyrs, teachers and heroes of faith. So why does the slogan 'Jesus is alive' offend Jews, if it asserts of him no more than may be asserted of any number of other dead people?

An obvious answer is that Jesus is thought of as being still *active* in the world. The highest spiritual authority and power are ascribed to him. Undoubtedly there are very acute intellectual difficulties in a claim of this kind. Arguments to the effect that some event in nature could have been brought about only by a specific supernatural cause and in no other way have been devastatingly criticized by philosophy since the time of Hume and Kant. And in any case, how could an argument of this type be brought forward to show that Jesus in particular is still active, without claiming as a corollary that what Jesus does can be distinguished from what God the Father does and from what the Spirit of God does – a claim which has long been considered heterodox? *Opera Trinitatis non ab extra divisa sunt*, goes the maxim. So both theology and philosophy would appear to rule out any argument of the form, 'Jesus must be alive, because only he could have done this.'

These considerations lead us, however, to a more substantial point. We see now that the slogan 'Jesus is alive' is not atomic or independent. As a matter of fact, if just those words are analysed we cannot reach an account of them which will either convince a philosopher, satisfy an orthodox Christian, or explain their offensiveness to the Jew. 'Jesus is alive' yields up its full meaning only when it is contextualized. We must examine the part the phrase plays with others in a whole doctrinal scheme and form of life, and what has been done with it historically. People who say that Jesus is alive are identifying themselves with an entire religious system, with a whole bundle of claims about Jesus and with a history. That history is a matter of pride to Christians, but the Jews have experienced the same history as a long-continued and crushing denial of their legitimacy, and therefore as a terrible history of religious conflict and suffering.

We began with what appeared to be a very simple and clear assertion – almost the sort of thing that Russell and the young Wittgenstein termed an 'atomic proposition'. We tried to do a bit of good old-fashioned philosophical analysis on it, and we soon discovered that religious meanings are *not* atomic or independent. Rather, the meaning of a particular religious phrase or slogan depends on the part it plays in a whole life-path and system of thought and on what has been done with it historically. We took a traditional philosophical question – 'What do these words mean?' – and by doing philosophy were soon led out of philosophy. We begin to see the point of the maxim that explanation in the human sciences has to be structural. If a person says 'Jesus is alive', and we want an interpretation or explanation of this bit of linguistic behaviour, then we will soon find that it can only be fully understood when it is set against the background of an entire cultural system or language-game (or whatever it be called). Just as you can explain the force and assess the merits of a particular chess move only if you invoke a lot of background knowledge of the whole game, its rules, its point, its theory and so on, so too you can explain 'Jesus is alive' only against the background of a lot of knowledge of Christianity, understood as a large body of slowly-evolving behavioural and linguistic conventions with a history, with various sub-species and so on. It is because we have this body of background knowledge that we know that the man who paid the Post Office to stamp 'JESUS IS ALIVE' on all those envelopes must have been an Evangelical businessman. Like putting Bibles in hotel bedrooms and scriptural texts on big posters in railway stations, it is exactly the sort of thing that Evangelical businessmen, and only they, do. And we know why they do these things: that is, we are familiar with their ideas about scriptural inspiration, language, the need to bear witness to one's faith and so on, all of which taken together explains why the man thought it would be a good thing to pay the Post Office £50,000 to stamp the slogan on the letters.

The example we have looked at has also given us a kind of potted history of philosophy generally, and of the philosophy of religion in particular, in the twentieth century. We began with 'literalism', an Anglicized version of traditional Aristotelean realism: true descriptive sentences are copies or representations or diagrams of things and their relationships out there in the world. Inspired by Frege and by new developments in symbolic logic, Russell attempted to construct an artificial language that would describe the world more literally and perspicuously than can be achieved even in the plainest of plain English:

> In a logically perfect language there will be one word and no more for every simple object, and everything that is not simple will be expressed by a combination of words, by a combination derived, of course, from the words for the simple things that enter in, one word for each simple component. A language of that sort will be completely analytic and will show at a glance the logical structure of the facts asserted or denied . . .[1]

Russell, in short, inspired twentieth-century British philosophy to aim at reaching a sublime degree of literalism, beyond the wildest dreams of the man on the Clapham omnibus. With such an ideal, and confronted by the sentence 'Jesus is alive', the philosopher of religion says to himself: 'This sentence seems to assert that out there in the world there's an individual who bears the name Jesus and who is alive and kicking. All we need to do is to fix how we are going to trace this man, check his identity and see if he's still getting around. It's basically the same job as verifying that Bob Hope is alive, and if it *isn't*, then the claim isn't factual at all.'

But we soon learnt that this straightforwardly realistic approach is too crude. I mean, just what do you do to track *Jesus* down and check if he's still breathing? Where do you look? So our position underwent certain changes as we realized that Jesus isn't quite thought of as being alive with a straightforwardly biological life, that the belief that he's still alive is a *religious* belief, that any life attributed to him may be thought real but if so must be non-natural, and that the confession of his aliveness springs from a whole complex religious system that lies behind it. We have moved from realism to non-realism. We started over half-a-century ago, with the idea that the religious slogan 'Jesus is alive' gets its justification or its warranted assertability from being an accurate representation of an extra-linguistic fact. Outside language, there's supposed to be a man who answers to the name of Jesus, and he's kicking yet. That's realism, but we had to drop it. Instead we were led to the view that the Christian religion as a whole is a large body of behavioural and linguistic conventions, and if you're a believer you're committed by these conventions to declaring that Jesus is alive.

So that is all there is: the short sentence 'Jesus is alive' gets its meaning and its warrant from its relation to a lot of other sentences in the system. The older sort of philosophical analysis broke down complex propositions into atomic ones, the idea being that the atomic propositions would report simple observations that anyone could check. Thus language was to be point-by-point mapped on to reality. But it all broke down as an account of descriptive language in general, and *a fortiori* it has broken down as an account of religious language. Religious doctrine itself insists that religious beliefs can't thus be checked out against the world empirically and point-by-point. God is never plainly presented to us in uninterpreted experience – if indeed there can be such a thing – and nor is Christ. All we ever have about them is text: canonical text, commentaries, secondary writings, rituals, linguistic idioms, rules about what can and can't be said – but in the end nothing is given but text text text. Religion is discourse only.

My learned critics attack me at this point by saying that either I haven't read or I haven't taken seriously this, that or the other writer or argument or consideration. So they refute my assertion that it is all text text text by chucking text text text at me, which leaves me at a loss to know how to reply. But if you don't like my idea of the ubiquity of language, would you please for the sake of consistency step forward and state your objection in some medium *other* than language? Thank you very much. Now keep a hold of that other medium, because I am going to ask you to use it again. You tell me you are a realist. At least sometimes, you say, we use language to talk about an order of things that's outside language and quite independent of it. Reality for you is two-layered: there is the world, and there is its representation in language. The two layers are asymmetrically related. Language tries to be *about* a world that is independent of it and doesn't need it. Thus the meaning of a sentence may be an objective state of affairs out there and quite independent of the sentence, and the objective truth-value of an assertion may be quite independent both of the steps anyone may take to determine it and also of whether anyone knows it or acts upon it. That's what we *mean* by objective truth and by realism. Meaning out there, truth out there, reality out there, facts out there; and language coming along second, trying to conform itself to what's out there.

Great. So you are confident that you know what is the relation between language and reality, between a true sentence and the objective fact of which it is true? You must tell me what this relation is; but if you try to give a true account *in language* of the relation between language and reality a vicious regress will open up. Your account in language of the language-reality relation (LRR), to be accurate, must already presuppose *its own* mastery of the LRR even as it sets out to determine the LRR. To avoid confusion on this point, you should employ some medium other than language in order to define the relation between true sentences in language and the states of affairs out there of which those sentences are a true report. And the medium you use will have to be able to compass *both ends* of the LRR.

I hope these last two paragraphs have made your head hurt. I am trying to convey the dizzying, abyssal character of the turn to language that began as far back as the 1930s, but whose full implications we have perhaps even yet not fully faced. In particular, the Enlightenment belief in the progressive rationalization of the world has come under threat. For two or three centuries it has been assumed that the historical process brings about a steady increase of knowledge, an advance of consciousness and so a progressively clearer view of the human situation, making possible the reform of all social institutions to make them more rational. Thus history becomes a progressive objectification of Reason. But most forms of this doctrine presuppose what we may call 'approximationism', by which I mean the notion that the representation of the world in our theories and our language can be brought into progressively clearer focus and so approximate more and more closely to the Truth. But this in turn presupposes the belief in absolute Truth, belief that the world is objectively a Cosmos independently of our knowledge of it, and belief in representation, that is, belief that our knowledge may more or less accurately portray or copy the way things really are. And as soon as we state these beliefs we see how dubious they are. How do we *make* all these comparisons? How do we know how the world is *apart* from our knowledge of it, so that we can compare the thing as represented in knowledge with the thing in itself, out of our knowledge? The very question is incoherent and nonsensical. The idea of truth is internal to our discursive practices, and external copying-truth is plainly mythical.

When we thus turn to language and begin to see our whole life as lived truly and fully inside our language, inside our culture, inside our knowledge-systems and inside our history, the dissolution of Enlightenment and Modernist ideology gathers pace. In particular I can no longer see myself as somehow sticking out of or transcending the cultural-linguistic world to which I belong and within which I am constituted. The culture-transcending autonomous individual subject – an observer who has taken a step back from the world in order to be able to see it more clearly, and who also by being thus a little disengaged is able to be an autonomous rational agent within the world – this subject, whom since Descartes we have purported to be, now comes under attack. I start to insist that I am immersed in my world, I am my own external relations, I am my life and there is no extrahistorical core of me that stands back from my life and observes it from outside.

The main themes of postmodernism thus become clear. They amount to a comprehensive rejection of virtually everything that the Enlightenment in general and Descartes in particular believed in. There is sharp criticism of the received ideas of representation, objective Truth, Reason and historical progress, leading eventually to 'the death of man', a thoroughly wholesome loss of interest in the individual subject, his self-mastery through self-consciousness, his moral autonomy and the justification of his knowledge of the world. Instead we turn more to language, the sign, communication, art and culture-criticism.

Although the beginnings of this shift are now traced by some back to the early nineteenth century, it is by no means universally popular. Anglo-Saxon thought in particular has been most reluctant to get itself up to date. Until not long ago we clung obstinately to an Early Modern conception of the task of philosophy as the justification of empirical knowledge. We felt ourselves on firm ground so long as we stuck close to logic, mathematics, the appeal to sense-experience and the scientific method, and in general to our traditional Cartesianism and empiricism. We largely eschewed questions of interpretation, social power, rhetoric, culture and historical change. Our idea was that *a priori* intellectual standards, sense experiences, the meanings of words, scientific knowledge and (most of all) philosophical writing could be objective, invariant, plain, lucid and error-free. We just didn't need to concern ourselves with all those murky topics that had preoccupied Continental philosophy since Hegel, infecting it with vagueness, politics, ranting and relativism. We had retained our intellectual virginity, and the pay-off was that – as we never ceased to remind ourselves – our standards of clarity and argumentative rigour were far higher than could be found across the Channel. We were very priggish, so much so that I am sorry to say that we were not very self-critical about our own much-vaunted clarity and rigour. We did not ask how they had been achieved, nor whether we had made a good bargain. For a price had of course been tacitly paid. We had followed Plato's path: an elite group, seduced by a rhetoric of the transcendence of rhetoric, had been led to think that they could outsoar the normal limitations of time and place and the pressures of power and the passions, and achieve a cool and godlike neutrality and precision of language and objectivity of knowledge. Again following Plato, the meanings of words and all our intellectual standards had been projected into the sky and made superhuman and (supposedly) independent of political interests and cultural change. No wonder we had all the sweet unshakable arrogance of a mandarin class.

As always in these matters I am describing an unspoken consensus among the second-rate rather than what was explicitly taught by the first-rate, but in any case the dam has now burst and philosophy is in turmoil. So far as all the varied movements of the day have a common theme, it is *anti-platonism*. Plato impressed upon the entire history of Western thought what now looks like a wholly unjustified and superstitious supernaturalism of thought, a supernaturalism of our intellectual standards, a supernaturalism of meanings (essentialism) and of knowledge, and finally *a supernaturalism of philosophy itself* – all of which has suddenly come to seem utterly absurd and unendurable. Nietzsche and Heidegger were right after all: Philosophy, capital-P Philosophy, had from the beginning been in headlong flight from time and from everything changeable; in flight from the earth, in flight from the body and the passions, in flight from biology and history. That is why, when I began to study philosophy at the end of the 1950s, the nineteenth century had been cut out of the syllabus. It was precisely during that century that a line of writers had demonstrated the ways in which human thinking is inevitably conditioned by history (Hegel), political interest (Marx), the passions and biology (Darwin, Nietzsche, Freud), culture (anthropology, leading up to Durkheim) – and so on. It was in the nineteenth century that language itself became a natural object whose history was put under the microscope, and just one page of the *Oxford English Dictionary* should have been enough to exorcise Plato forever. But we did not wish to think about what the historicality of language and conceptual change might imply for philosophy. So we avoided the nineteenth century and pretended we were not in history.

Yet just a page of the *OED* shows that we cannot utter timeless truths, for we have no timeless vocabulary. Just one page of the *OED* shows how completely language – I mean, the way sentences are put together, and the meaning of every word – is always tied to the preoccupations and the demands of some particular historical period. For the whole of our life, including our standards, is intrahistorical. Slowly each thing shifts: nothing is fixed, so everything becomes a period piece. History has no outside and is not going anywhere; its development is just immanent and not relative to anything outside it. The whole is so unbounded in every way – that there *is* no Whole.

Everything is utterly unfounded, and we float on a boundless heaving ocean of interrelated contingencies. Language is just a human improvisation. We use it to coordinate our activities and so to cope with our world. But nothing in language is tied down or permanently compelled to be the way it is. The meaning of a word is rather like the price of a stock in a market, a relative shifting thing that is the resultant of a very large number of small human interactions. There can no more be an absolute meaning than there can be an absolute price. Words are just what is currently being done with them. And we are always inside the language in which our current vision of the world is embodied. We never actually get right outside language so that we can directly inspect the language-reality relation. There isn't anywhere outside language to be got to. So once again, the implication is that we are not anything that could be lifted out of the flux: I just am my life, my external relations and the language I hear and produce. I can no more be lifted out of history than a wave can be lifted from the sea. Again, the implication is that everything is constituted within the foundationless, unanchored, evolving cultural-linguistic whole of which we are all part and to which we all contribute.

As seen from the point of view of Western thought, we are currently engaged in 'historicizing epistemology'. We don't seek to *justify* knowledge-claims. We merely contextualize them. As Nietzsche insisted must be done henceforth, all intellectual expressions, all human outputs, need to be related to the historical-social circumstances of their production in order to be understood aright.[2] So we are now thoroughgoing pluralists and historical relativists. From the Eastern standpoint it may seem that we have adopted something very close to the Buddhist metaphysics that sees reality as a boundless swarm of minute, insubstantial reciprocally-conditioning events, with no necessity, foundation or Goal anywhere. The main difference is that for 'events' we read 'signs', with an accompanying emphasis on the automotive, self-proliferating properties of signs. But we do indeed resemble Buddhism now in recognizing as mythological the ways in which most other systems of thought have attempted to defer the Void. That is to say, I, Don Cupitt, am at this present instant no more than a bunch of pure defenceless contingencies breasting absolute Nothingness. I am right up against Nothingness and unshielded from it. But most people cannot endure the thought of what they call meaninglessness or irrationality. They make up ideas that defer the Void. So the world rests upon the back of an elephant, which stands on the back of a tortoise, and so on. More philosophically, people try to give the world an underlying intellectual structure to help fend off the Void. Thus contingent particulars are made to seem a bit more solid by being grounded in universals, laws, necessities and the like. People like to picture the world as having an absolute Beginning, Ground and Destiny. And such ideas may quite genuinely help us to face the world and cope with life, so that they are not altogether to be despised. However, they are mythological, we made them, and though they may keep the Void at bay for a while they cannot finally overcome it.

The postmodern Christian further agrees with the Buddhist that true religion and the way to peace of mind is *not* by building up and reinforcing our dogmatic defences against the Void, but by actually running to it and embracing it. Like Christ going voluntarily to his end, we should accept the Void. When we have welcomed it in, it cannot frighten us any more.

As for philosophy, it clearly now becomes interpretative, unsystematic and conversational, not foundational. We forget all superstitious ideas of absolute standards, values, certainties or truths. We forget ideas of another world. Everything is contingent, and necessity is just conventional. There is nothing but changing customs. Since we never get out of language and culture, which are made of signs which in turn are all of them unanchored and changing all the time, we see that nothing is pure, atomic and sheerly-given. Interpretation goes all the way down. We have to learn to think in a new way: the public cultural world of meaning comes first, society precedes the individual and culture precedes nature. Everything is immersed in, everything floats on, everything is part of the boundless, glittering, heaving Sea of Meanings.

However, a crisis develops when I realize that everything I have just been writing has refuted itself by relying upon the very Logos that it attacks. This time I am going to charge down this question of self-reflexivity. Let's go to the limit in demythologizing reason itself, see where we get to, and only *then* vex ourselves with the question of our warrant for doing something so self-contradictory.

(b) Sex, power and the production of reason

An English idiom reminds us that 'the facts of life' which a child needs first to understand are those concerned with the mystery of sex. Why are there two sexes, what is the relation between them, and what is the meaning for my life of the fact that I am assigned to this sex or to that?

The male is perceived by the child as being the larger and physically stronger of the two sexes, his superior activity and dominance being associated with his better control over what passes through his bodily orifices. He is active, not passive: he invades, he doesn't get invaded. *Passive* homosexuality, a taste for getting invaded, is commonly regarded as very shameful in a man by societies which have not the least objection to active homosexuality. As for the connection between bodily integrity and strength of identity, it is notable that there are peoples among whom it is denied that adult, initiated male warriors shit. Athletics and war may require temporary continence. Western monks pray nightly to be delivered from polluting nocturnal emissions. The bodily orifices of corpses are sealed and plugged – I've done it – presumably to diminish their fearsome unholiness. In general, a man is pure, strong and holy insofar as he is *sealed up*. Bits must not fall off or leak away.

If we live in 'a man's world', it would seem that reality itself favours and privileges that which is relatively more unified, substantial, self-identical, active, integral, closed, independent, self-consistent and systematically coherent – i.e., more like God. For consider by contrast the plight of woman as perceived by the child. She appears to be less strong, less independent and with a weaker identity. Her body is cloven by a wound that drips blood monthly. Her ritual purity and integrity, that is, her identity, is further ruptured by the invasions of men and her own extrusions of babies. She is accordingly seen as being a relatively more impure, fickle, leaky, unstable and vulnerable creature who needs protection and control. If however she were celibate, and even more if she were to fast so much that her periods stopped, then (in late ancient times) she had some hope of becoming 'as perfect as a man'.

The male-female relation is therefore viewed and symbolized as a relation between a dominant term which is relatively light, stable, closed up, exalted, strong, self-identical and self-consistent, and its opposite, its counterpart, its excluded, subordinate, unstable, protean Other. Because symbolically man is relatively unchanging and woman is changeable, the almost infinite number of permutations that the male-female relation goes through are chiefly changes in the female term. At a wedding we all watch the bride. The ritual focusses around her because she's the one to whom most happens. She is more *interesting*; women undergo more profound changes than men do.

Now man is to woman as reason is to the passions. Reason is the dominance of the masculine principle; reason is the fact that the world is so ordered (or it is our task so to order it) as to privilege unity and self-sameness. Independence, changelessness, self-consistency and systematic unity – all this just *is* rationality and *is* masculinity. It is the masculine principle that demands order, systematization, coherence and 'closure', or rounding off, in bodies of knowledge, works of art, and history itself. Further, the asymmetry of the man-woman relation is elegantly reflected by, and put through various permutations in, the founding distinctions of Philosophy: form and matter, the necessary and the contingent, the universal and the particular, being and becoming, the eternal and the temporal, subject and predicate and so on.

Something rather more than mere symbolic correspondence was involved in all this. Consider the form-matter distinction, which Derrida regards as 'opening philosophy'. Every physical thing is made of form and matter, including a human baby. It seemed appropriate to ancient biology that all the matter of a baby should be supplied by the mother. Matter is seen as female-type stuff, made of pairs of opposed qualities, unstable and ambivalent like the passions. The matter of a baby therefore consisted of nine menstrual discharges duly saved up. The father for his part provided the baby's form. Form is spiritual and intellectual, and the semen is an immaterial formative agency. Form rules and orders matter.

It follows therefore that the form-matter/male-female parallel is a good deal more than metaphorical. The connexion between God, masculinity, form and the rational soul (the form of the body) on the one hand, and between woman, matter and corruptibility on the other was built into philosophy, science and theology at their inception. It is undeniable that Western thought from the beginning has been applied sexism. The Greeks made no bones about it. The sun's rays had a fertilizing and formative power in them that made living things sprout from the earth, *exactly* as semen made woman fruitful.[3] Both were cases of the action of form upon matter. The Form of the Good and the 'Spermatic Logos' were spoken of in similar terms. They formed all things just as semen forms a child, and the power in semen was therefore a sacred and heavenly power.[4]

So man's domination of woman provided the basic pattern in which thought operated, and when put through a number of permutations was the model for the construction of the Universe. The case of sexism reveals the extent to which Philosophy was as mythological as the older religious ways of thinking that it purported to displace. Philosophy was just abstract and depersonalized mythology. The male continued to be the active, spiritual, intellectual, creative, fructifying and controlling principle, and the woman was the subordinate, passive, receptive, earthy and fruitful principle. They were related as line to colour, melody to harmony, pattern to stuff and so on, and between them they gave birth to all things.

Systematization and unification was achieved by the operation of another principle which decreed that in the Great Chain of Being everything was relatively submissive and feminine in relation to what was above it in rank, and relatively dominant and masculine vis-à-vis what was below it. Men who have met the Queen will recall that they had to wait for her to speak first, and there are many historical examples of women sovereigns taking on distinctly masculine behavioural traits. The rule is that a servant bears witness to the superior's vastly greater power by being silent, immobile, attentive and deferential, with downcast eyes but ready to spring into action when called upon. He or she may be compelled to live in a state of physical seclusion and perhaps celibacy. Footmen, monks and nuns, Muslim women, and courtiers were required to be like this, in a way that might override the biological sex of the parties involved. As Supermale, God requires us all to be still and wait upon him.

So we have two general principles. The first is the male-female/form-matter principle, which goes through a number of different permutations, and the second is the principle of gender-relativity in a graded or rank-ordered system. Put these principles together and give them free rein, and they will generate a complete vision of the universe. In particular, of course, they will produce belief in one God as the male of males, lordly, active and creative, spiritual and supreme in perfection, power and wisdom. God is so great that he takes over the creativity of both sexes. By creating the rational soul himself he makes the human male redundant, and by not needing any female consort to help him create, and instead requiring the cultural denial of female sexuality and the concealment of the female reproductive system, he makes the female redundant. God annuls sexual creativity, thus leading people to say that it is *he* who has made every one of us. In the same way God takes over all truth, for he constitutes and himself just is the one compulsory Truth of all things and the one basis of the moral world-order. God is thus the Centre, Apex or Coping-Stone, that upon which all the hierarchies converge and which holds everything together.

Rationalism, monotheism and male supremacy are perhaps most strikingly synthesized in Islam. There, the duty continually to reaffirm the unity of God is the duty to hold strictly together and to equate with each other a large number of themes which might otherwise begin to slip apart just a little. And they must *not* slip apart, even by so much as a hairsbreadth. A Muslim must maintain undiminished the spiritual supremacy, self-sufficiency and holiness of the masculine principle, the moral order in society, his own honour, the virtue and good reputation of his womenfolk, his own protection of them therefore, and his control over them – and the key idea of 'strictness' in monotheistic faith and practice means that control depends upon keeping these various themes in perfect coincidence and equivalence with each other. That is what it is to believe in one God.[5]

But although Islam illustrates the main points most clearly, the modern West still provides abundant examples of the complex of ideas involved here. Whether you are a physicist or a physician or whatever, you will know that in your field the strong men, the guardians, equate Reason with discipline, stability, formality, control, objectivism, law and order, and a clear chain of command. So, in effect, everything must be systematically ordered and unified under one supreme Principle or authority. When that is achieved, we know where we are. More than women, it seems, men need Power, and the completest expression of their Power is what they call Reason. The doctrine of Reason is the ideology of male supremacy.

Insofar as in these past few pages we have presented a very brief account of how a certain circle of ideas hang together – a descriptive account – we have not I hope transgressed the bounds of masculine reason. The ideas were sketched immanently, without being attacked head-on. They were given only the slightest colouring, intended (if you are inclined that way) to hint obliquely at how *odd* all this is and how inevitably it is now slipping into the past tense. There would be an obvious reflexive difficulty in a clear and systematic demonstration of the crazy repressiveness of the ideas of clarity and system, but it is surely not necessary to go quite as far as that. It is sufficient to allow our writing, including philosophical writing, to become gradually more relaxed, plural, 'feminine' and art-like, in the style of the Nietzschean maxim that 'Truth is a woman'.[6]

The question of monotheism is trickier. Is feminism going to be the death of God? It appears to be difficult for people to conceive of any transcendent and controlling Person being as other than just masculine. Man is sameness, woman is difference: because the Transcendent is always unifying and Selfsame it has to be called masculine. Feminists who have attempted to revive a Goddess-cult seem themselves to link her with Nature. Neuter pronouns in association with God may suggest a somewhat sinister and possibly-malignant impersonality. A mix of masculine and feminine pronouns has not been tried and is almost certainly unworkable.

I once wrote a short theological book which avoided using *any* gender-suggesting pronouns or titles in connection with God. The idea was that I would try to convey that God was personal but mysterious and transcendent, and neither masculine nor feminine. The first reviewer, a Christian, reacted by describing the work as 'perhaps the most heterodox book ever published by an Anglican clergyman', and concluded that I had evidently lost belief in the personality of God. This meant that in his view there can be no non-sexual person, not even a Divine one, and that religion for Christians as much as for Muslims is first and foremost about the symbolization and social control of sexuality. A theological book whose pronouns and other anthropo-morphisms are *not* giving on every page a stream of coded information about the cosmic significance of human sexual dimorphism, and directions about the control of heterosexual relations, is an utterly useless and heretical book. So my reviewer's reaction showed the extent to which even today orthodoxy is just sexism and sexism is orthodoxy. In which case indeed Christian feminism represents a major internal revolution in Christianity that must eventually bring about the death of the old God. Feminism represents a revolt of the radically plural, humanist and libertarian strand in Christianity against the punishing repressive force of selfsame patriarchal reason.

Deconstruction suggests a number of ways in which God can be turned against God, and masculine reason can be destabilized from within. First, we can exploit the internal oppositions and polarities that are to be found among the well-established doctrinal themes. For example, we can, like Bonhoeffer, contrast the world-controlling power of God manifest in the creation-theme with the weakness of God manifest in the story of the crucifixion.[7] Secondly, we can demonstrate that even those theologians who are at first sight the most alienated, power-hungry, authoritarian and literalist in outlook have, nevertheless, and in spite of themselves, produced texts that are very writerly, metaphorical, fictive and exegetically imaginative. Calvin is the most obvious example. He claims to be a literalist, but in fact has invented his theology. His exegesis is wayward and wilful even as he says that it must not be so. Thirdly, we can undermine repressive, monistic, controlling Reason in a most polite manner by pretending to act as its interpreters and spokesmen. We may just explain it on its own terms and in a manner to which it cannot possibly take exception – and that, *just that*, can today be quite sufficient refutation of it.

I am not retracting the view that rationality is sexist. Hitherto, men have made the rules and have defined reality. They have defined woman as different, anarchic and lacking in due respect for social order and hierarchy. Uncontrolled, she is a threat, but when she is controlled you can be sure who your own children are. Lineages become recognizable with confidence, the kinship-system settles down, and the orderly transmission of property down the line is made possible. In that sense man's secure, rightful, jealous and exclusive possession of woman and her fruit becomes not just a metaphor for, but also the psycho-logical key to, all other possession.[8] And only when woman (and sex, and reproduction, and kinship) has thus been got under control can there be an orderly system of rights and duties. Only then do you know who your own folk are, and only then can you assess the relative strengths of different claims upon you. So, once again, the subjection of woman has historically been the key to morality, social order, and culture generally.

Form and matter, the ruling principle and that which must be ruled, male and female – reason grew out of all this. Interestingly, it grew out of sexism, that is, out of precisely that area in which we are all of us most obdurately blind and unreasonable. We don't know how to change it at a deep level, and indeed the very notion of changing it is perhaps incoherent (at least in terms of the logic of sameness). But in a high civilization such as ours, when the feminine comes forward we also become more aware of the devices by which women have survived under male rule and have even fought back against it. An all-out revolutionary overthrow of Reason is unthinkable, but women have historically found ways of *outwitting men at their own game*. These wiles and guiles and devices, this cunning and irony, this turning of the opponent's own strength back against him, is related to masculine reason as (in the mediaeval trivium) rhetoric is to logic, and just at present it is of the very highest philosophical interest.[9] A number of the most original and creative modern philosophers (including Nietzsche, Wittgenstein and Derrida) have been rediscovering rhetoric and using its wiles against blundering one-eyed theoretical reason.

This is a very promising line of approach, and it suggests that we may after all be able to make the transition to less mystifying, less privileged and less sexist conceptions of reason and of God.

(c) Religion after Truth

It may be possible, then, to move away from the traditional Western supernaturalism of selfsame masculine Reason. We can acknowledge that our thinking, our logic and our rationality are not 'pure' but are always intertwined with – and originally were actually produced by – the requirements of sex, power and other practical interests. We will adjust more easily to this realization if our philosophical writing, especially in England, can give up its somewhat naïve scientism. It needs to become more aware, humorous, plural, subversive, rhetorical and 'feminine'.

What of the corresponding move in the case of religion? For one thing, the very notion of an *orthodoxy*, a crowd-truth imposed by authority that must be believed in standard form as a matter of discipline, is surely in the highest degree stupid and 'masculine'. What I am calling 'rhetoric' will undermine it by showing that the attempt to master meaning and enforce a fixed compulsory crowd-truth will always be defeated by the endlessness of interpretation. To understand we must interpret, and interpretation is historically-conditioned and endlessly variable. It cannot be controlled. If the idea of a church is logically tied to the idea of a fully-defined system of tenets to be understood in exactly the same way by everyone, then the church is dead. But fortunately there are no essences and no indissoluble logical bonds. Nothing has to be thought of as unalterable. Analyticity is merely conventional, and conventions can be changed. At present, many or most people think there can't possibly be a church without literalism and a ponderous one-eyed masculine attempt to pin down meaning and truth. We'll have to persuade them to start thinking differently. We'll have to show that there cannot be a fully common truth because meaning cannot be fully mastered. Would-be ideological tyrannies can never wholly succeed in achieving their goal of enslaving us because they cannot completely fix meaning. That puts an end to orthodoxy.

More difficult is the task of unmasking and renouncing a certain supernaturalism of religion. There is – it seems we must say – no pure and autonomous essence of religion or category of the religious on which we can safely take our stand. On the contrary, religion has been very varied historically, and often we have strong grounds for suspecting that its latent content is something quite different from its manifest content. The possibility that in any particular case this may already be so, or may be quietly getting to be so without our realizing it, has a devastating effect on theology. Especially for those of us who are by temperament highly religious, it is disquieting to reflect that there is no guarantee of the innocence and transparency of religion. Perhaps our religious feelings were once relatively innocent, but have ceased to be so without our being aware of it? We cannot tell for sure.

The examples are painful to produce. One world faith seems to me, I can't help it, to be effectively about little else but sexism, oppression and reaction. A thousand years ago it produced great art and mysticism. Is one to say that things were different then, and that the meaning of the faith has changed without the faithful being aware of it? Or, if that sounds too much as if we are postulating an objective meaning and truth of things, then perhaps we should say that new discourses have been developed in the modern period whose influence has meant that where other people once saw holiness and piety, we can now see only mindless repression and cruelty.

Another case, nearer home. A friend longs for 'Early Service' according to the *Book of Common Prayer* in a mediaeval country church on a cool bright summer's morning. Is this a truly religious longing for the recovery of childhood faith and a lost Paradise, or is it merely right-wing politics seeking to restore a peaceful graded social order in which all know their place? Either interpretation is possible, and there is no Truth. There isn't any point of view from which one of these two interpretations could be vindicated and shown to be right, and the other to be wrong. We have to live with interminable ambiguity in a way that undoes all traditional ideas of uncompromised authenticity, purity, holiness and innocence. There are no longer any saints without warts.

Thus we have the difficult problem of coming to terms with the de-centering of theology, that is, with the realization that there cannot be any guarantee that theology is about what it thinks it's about and is able to keep itself about what it thinks it's about. At any time a new Marx, or a new Freud or a feminist may come along and develop a new style of interpretation that completely alters the way we read a theological text. Meaning cannot be held still or protected against sudden displacement from outside.

The de-centering of religion presents me with a familiar problem. As has happened so often before, I have to recant my own views of a few years ago. That's the story of my life – recantations. Especially around 1979–1981, I was preoccupied with the idea of defining the essence of the religious, as if 'the religious' as a category were an autonomous, pure and timeless essence that could be relied upon. My idea was that when I had discovered it I would use it as a touchstone for the criticism of theology. Kant had done a moral critique of theology, so I would attempt a religious one.

Kant, 'the last Deist', was still a kind of platonist who believed that he could pin down an *a priori* essence of the moral. But morality and religion are not platonic essences; they are mere historical formations. They change. And what else can one conclude from this elementary observation but that it is up to us and us alone to invent for our own time new and interesting moral and religious forms?

From the past history of the concept of religion four main uses are worth recalling. In antiquity, religion (*hosiotes*, *eusebia*, *pietas*, *religio*) could mean the punctilious performance of all prescribed rituals, due respect and reverence towards sacred beings, persons and customs, and right conduct generally. In the later very other-worldly culture of Christian neoplatonism religion could mean a yearning for Yonder. Homesick people lamented their exile in this transient and worthless life of ours, and longed for death and the heavenly world above. In later mediaeval times religion meant a particular social zone: it was the sum of all the spaces and spheres and forms of life that were directly subject to ecclesiastical law only. You entered religion by special rites and vows, and all permanent inhabitants of the religious realm lived under rule. Finally, in modern times (that is, since the Enlightenment) *a* religion has come to be seen as something like a language, an ideology, a culture, or even an *ethnē*. It is a large-scale objective social system of beliefs and practices to which individuals may or may not happen to belong. You can opt in or opt out of the community.

The view that a religion is a 'creed' is typically Christian, as indeed the word implies. Though modern, its origins doubtless go back to early times, when faith was gradually turned into '*the* Faith'. But it has become particularly salient since the late Middle Ages, its canonization being encouraged by the pressure of church authority, the spread of printed Bibles and 'literalism', and the desire to emulate scientific realism. The Reformation Confessions of Faith turned Christian belief into something like a political ideology. This facilitated the emergence in the sixteenth century of the repellent use of the word 'creed' to mean merely a set of tenets on any subject whatever. Finally, in the Enlightenment other regional traditions of faith were named and described as 'religions' and so became also 'creeds'.

Thus religion began as a disposition of the soul and a virtue, but became steadily more objectified and intellectualized until in the end it was a great institution and a set of tenets.[10] The Western church in particular gradually developed into a totalitarian society, a persecuting absolute ideological monarchy. But the complex historical process by which it had reached this condition told against the claims it made when in it. For the process showed that texts are interpreted variously in different periods and that religion changes. It certainly cannot be systematized or totalized diachronically, but nor can religion be systematized even synchronically, for at any one time it will be found to be multidimensional. That is, it contains many diametrically-opposed tendencies that pull in opposite directions, and so can skew the entire interpretation of faith in one way or another. Thus it may be world-affirming or world-denying, it may be God-centred or Christ-centred, rationalist or voluntarist, catholic and inclusive or rigorist, sectarian and exclusive. Religion may at one extreme be equated with concern for ritual purity, or at the other extreme become purely ethical. The believer may be a solitary quietist, or given over to militant communal activism. The dominant religious style may be centralist and hierarchical, or it may be centrifugal and dispersed.

From all this – from the unmasterability of meaning, the endlessness of interpretation and the futility therefore of attempting to maintain central control of truth, and from the multidimensionality and the sheer diversity of religion both diachronically and synchronically – it follows that a religious tradition is an object somewhat like a culture or a language.[11] To attempt to totalize or systematize it is to misunderstand it. The relation of the believer to the tradition in which she stands is more like the relation between competence and performance in Chomsky's account of language. A religion, considered as a complex social fact, is not the sort of thing that can usefully be called true or false. It is more like a game or a language. It needs to be learnt by practice. We steep ourselves in it, become skilled or competent, and then when we know the vocabulary and the idioms we can start to put on our own performance. The community-tradition has given us a vocabulary, and in it we now frame our own personal life-project.

The reason why we need this is that human beings live in a world of signs. We can act only in a language. Indeed, we are *made* of signs. We just *are* our lives, that is, our external relations, that is, the sum of all the symbolic communication that passes through us. We are constituted within the vocabularies that we live by, which is why we get a new name at baptism. Unlike animals we don't just live; we have to live meaningfully, through signs. My religion as a Christian, then, is the sign-system within which my identity is constituted and through which I live my life.

Christianity as a great river of signs isn't true in the sense of being *about* anything other than itself. Signification is always sideways and differential – which is why it moves and keeps on moving. Any attempt to anchor the sign, either to a transcendent signified right outside language or to a transcendental signified (a meaning or a thought) on the near side of language, is a mistake. If there was depth I'd call it a very deep mistake, the mistake of supposing that you can do language a bit of good by stopping its movement, by mooring it to a fixed point outside it. Sorry; no. Language has got to be able to float free and move, in order to *be* language. Without that moving, free-floating quality that frightens us so much and which we seek to deny, language would not work and we could not live in it in the way we do.[12]

So truth doesn't consist in a relation between chains of signs and something else external to language. When I say that Christianity is true I mean that this particular system of signs and house of meaning is trustworthy and reliable as a medium and a vocabulary in which I can frame my own religious life. Christ the Word is truth, that's all. We do not need more than that, and there is no more to it than that. For popular old-style objective Truth rested on the mythical idea of an isomorphism or pre-established harmony between two distinct realms, that of signs and that of things. The idea was first that the former could somehow copy and convey the latter, and secondly that its fidelity or accuracy in this copying could be checked. But in fact the world only takes on a definite shape through our organizing activity, as we wrap it up in language. It is chaos made cosmos by language, or rather, first appears as cosmos *in* language. So there aren't two orders which can be compared with each other, but only one.

This means that we should give up thinking in terms of a compulsory, permanent, extra-mental Truth of things. There is only our own ever-changing historical production. No matter: we can still be utterly committed like artists to our own vocation, to our own contingent beliefs, values and life-project. And the religion I make up for myself, my personal Christian-life-project, can be evaluated aesthetically. As we have insisted, there is no fixed and reliable publicly-available yardstick for assessing religion. Neither an immutable fully-defined orthodoxy nor a pure essence of the religious is available to us any more. But like a work of literature, my Christian-life-project can be contextualized within the tradition to which it belongs, and against that background it can be judged aesthetically.

(d) Theological fragments

Theology in the past has sought to achieve masculine sameness, that is, communal and official control of meaning and systematization of truth. Standardization of truth at the public level secures uniformity in subjection at the private level. So the chief truth that theology needs to establish is that the individual desperately needs something on which the community in general and its officers in particular have the exclusive franchise. The doctrine is fourfold: you need it urgently, they alone can supply what you need, they are fully authorized to supply to you the genuine article, one-hundred-per-cent pure; and therefore you must be subject to them. You didn't imagine that they would just *give* it away, did you?

Thus theology is about spiritual power and subjection to spiritual power, and has been so since St Paul. Elaborating the early Christian message against the background of the Old Testament and the Jewish sacred history, Paul is concerned to legitimate the infant gentile church in its struggle with the synagogue. At a second level he must demonstrate his own authority to propound this teaching, so he seeks to show the legitimacy of his own apostolic commission.

Just the same themes are developed in later Christianity. You could rely on what the church purveyed because its ministrations were controlled by the bishop, who was certified a true successor of the apostles, who had been personally commissioned by Christ, who himself was nothing less than the plenitude of God incarnate. Thus the water of life flowed straight down the pipeline from the highest heaven into your ears and into your open mouth, and dogma guaranteed that there had been no loss or contamination in the process of transmission.

Early in the thirteenth century, theology became a university subject, and was at once turned into a grandiose systematic science. The old theme of defining the right channels through which you could attain the right sort of knowledge of the right God was kept, but incorporated into a wider version of theology as cosmic myth, history of redemption, ruling truth-power, encyclopaedia of answers to (as it seemed) almost every urgent practical and speculative question – and, last but not least, backing for the power of a persecuting church.

From that era of the church's highest confidence and worldly grandeur – from, perhaps, 1200 to 1650 – later Christianity inherited a tendency to see authoritarianism as orthodox. To this day in what people say about the church and religion there remains a presumption in favour of centralized authority, objective truth, ecclesiastical order and discipline, and mastery in exercising control first over oneself and then over others. There is still a strong preference for a structured cosmos, a ready-made world-order, and for both God and the soul to be, as one might put it, strong Egos. That is, God and his finite counterpart the Self should both be centred, substantial and self-present, in the sense of having full and simultaneous self-knowledge and self-posses-sion. We seem to assume the worshipfulness of a boundless will-to-power which, though almighty, needs more yet. Further, we are biased towards an account of religious truth that sees it as coming down to us from Above, timeless, certain, ready-made, given and immutable.

So deeply do we take all this for granted that we were largely unaware of it until it was all called into question. *Then* we could begin to ask ourselves why we suppose that it is possible or even desirable to systematize or totalize every aspect of the world and of our lives around a single Centre and under the rule of a single Monarch. Why does God have to be such intensely centralized and concentrated Power? Why do we so much wish to privilege Unity, selfsameness and presence? On the face of it, it would seem that spiritual freedom calls for plurality and diversity *without* everything getting unified under a single controlling authority, so that a religion of spiritual liberation should have an anti-systematic and centrifugal theology. Besides, does it make sense to suppose that our human life can be systematically unified? *Dasein*, human existence, is extended in time and the successive-ness of life destroys system. Even at the very simplest level, I am not grown up enough to make a unitary plan for my life until over a fifth of it is already past, and then, supposing that in adolescence or young adulthood I make a coherent life-plan, even so, during the decades that follow the world will change, I will change and my plan will change. If you are not yet aware of the way the decades change your values and your life-plan even as you live it out, then you will be, you will be.

Our life cannot have a single pre-planned meaning because life is always historical, multifarious and inter-subjective, embedded in culture and vulnerable to mischances. I had a life-plan once, but as I set out to enact it it began to change continuously and uncontrollably. I stuck to the task, because that is easy. But I could not maintain a fixed conception of what the task *was*. We cannot stop beliefs, values and meanings from changing over time. That is why the meaning of a life cannot be fully systematized or totalized. It is capable only of a narrative or an artistic kind of unification. But that kind of art-unity is variable and ambiguous, wide open to any number of new angles and interpretations that may come along at any time. In a human life, art-unity is the only sort of unity we can realize. I think it is enough; but it is not systematic or scientific.[13]

As with my life, so too with the cosmos. We live in a highly plastic, multifaith world in which individuals and entire cultures may flourish within any of an indefinitely wide range of mythologies, symbolizations and world-visions. The attempt to privilege one of them cannot be more than a bit of local self-assertion, on a par with claiming that God talks Arabic and not Hebrew, or vice versa.

Our systematic theology then has been the product of a will to power and a celebration of the hungry ego. Our privileging of absolute Unity, selfsameness and presence has posited a Subjectivity completely present and perspicuous to itself, quite inexhaustibly interested in itself and keen to dramatize itself, untiringly seeking to extend and elaborate its power over souls and instantly blaming and striving to overcome anything that remains obdurately different from itself. In Western thought it has been supposed that God, the old men in the Vatican, kings, potentates, patriarchs – in a word, all ruling egos – were like this. Indeed, precisely this mentality's ceaseless celebration of its own mystique and radiation of its own glory was the basis of the values of the West, political, ethical and religious. And when I speak of a fragmentary and post-Western theology, I mean a religious outlook that has completely left behind the West's traditional religion of the *monstre sacré*, insatiable egoism and will-to-power.

Instead, a fully-modernized religious outlook will *first of all* be wholly this-worldly. It will have given up the habit, common to Plato and to religious supernaturalism, of looking to a higher world for explanations, legitimations, standards, compensations and the rest. No: that is all gone. Standards and certainties of that type cannot now be restored. We shall have to learn to look only sideways, and not jump to any higher occult realm. We must confine ourselves to the horizontal diversification, elaboration and unfolding of our imagery and our practices.

Language is a living, moving, continuous and wholly imma-nent thing, a human improvisation completely bound up with the daily interactions, practices and games that it facilitates and furthers. All of language has to be free to heave and move together, as it must be possible for a single breaker to roll across the entire breadth of the ocean. There are no gaps in the sea, and no bit of the sea can be moored. In order to work a natural language has to be as continuous and mobile as that, and therefore there is no way in which a bit of language, a certain tract of it, can be tied into a higher, unchanging and extra-human world.

Secondly, it follows from this that the Christian must now be beliefless. We do not know how any beliefs about supernatural beings, powers or the like could be rational. Adrift on the open sea of meaning we no longer have any absolute Beginning, End, foundation, anchorage or Centre. There is nothing fixed, atomic or eternal. And although naturally I understand belief as involving a moral rather than an intellectual allegiance to the Christian community and its tradition, so that faith is for me a practical decision to live through a certain symbolic and ethical vocabulary, I have to admit that even this undogmatic and ethical type of religion is just as much subject to historical change as a more dogmatic faith. There is no permanent essence of Christian-ity, however minimal, because there are no essences. Nothing's fixed: *really* nothing's fixed. Instead the Christian is emptied-out, free-floating, anonymous in the flux of life with no special privileges or secret knowledge whatever, a penniless vagrant now and free. This condition is the traditional *kenosis*, the emptied-out-ness, poverty and nakedness of Christ. Since a Christian is a person for whom the world has already ended, we above all others should be able to cope with the end of the West. Losing our faith, losing *everything*, we draw close to Christ. Dammit, 'orthodox Christianity' was the oxymoron all the time! Culture-Christianity, propping up civilization, always was an absurdity. It made people forget that the central symbol of the faith is an image of dereliction and loss; the true faith is the loss of faith. The orthodox are the real heretics in this strange world, where the outside is the real inside and the poorest are the richest.

Thirdly, faith must now be mobile. Truth is not the position you hold but the path you tread, a path without a destination and whose course is unpredictable. In the days of the old agriculture-based peasant cultures lifelong allegiance to a fixed dogmatic faith came as naturally as the unchanging cycles of the seasons and the liturgical year. But nowadays reality changes continuously and we with it. Everything is all the time up for redesigning, including us and our faith. Everything is ephemeral. Theology therefore goes symbolist and sets about reinterpreting, improvising and reinventing itself non-stop. We abandon the traditional notion of a deposit of faith to be guarded like treasure, and instead we think of truth as something that has to be created continuously. Nor need we become boring by yet again quoting art as a parallel; let us instead quote physics. At school and even at first-degree level people may fancy that modern physics is a body of objective knowledge. But 'objective knowledge' is a vulgarization, a notion appropriate for journalism and quiz programmes. At the leading edge where the real action is, there is nothing but a running debate. After attending to the arguments for a while you may feel able to report that the stock of some theories seems to be rising and the stock of other theories seems presently to be falling. But obviously the subject would die if general agreement were ever to be reached and the arguments were accordingly to cease. So the subject lives only so long as 'objective knowledge' is precisely *not* attained, but remains a mirage. Truth must forever be a running argument and a continuing process of production, and it can never become a settled conclusion. We should forget about conclusions. Conclusion does not happen. We never reach it.

Fourthly, then, faith has to be creative. We must learn to do without any objective truth, without a developed cosmology, without ideology, without progress or destination. Instead we should learn to love just the struggle, the movement, the continual process of production, the running argument and the work – a work which is always *labor* and never *opus*, for there is no finished product. Faith is to love, beautiful word, the *fray*. Too much of pre-Enlightenment faith was dogma-guided yearning for the world above, an impotent lament. But what's Christian about spending your whole life fancying you are in a state of exile and wishing to be somewhere else? Those who thus wanted to be finished and out of the fray were merely in love with death. Death is the one and only capital-T Truth, for to long for certainty, for completion, for an End, for an arrival, is merely to long for death.

So *finally* our anti-theology must say Yes to contingency and dispersal. The fluid postmodern vision of the world dissolves away all substances, including the Cosmos, the Self and God as they were traditionally understood. Instead of seeing God, Christ and the Self as immortal spiritual substances, self-possessed and self-asserting, we see them instead on the model of creative self-giving. Powerless, they continually pass out into plurality. (Incidentally, in the English-speaking world we tend to discuss the question of God rather crudely along just one axis, existence-nonexistence. But it is in many contexts more profitable to conduct the debate along other axes, including especially the biblical power-weakness, and the 'French' centred-dispersed.) In antiquity there was a notion of God as being so exalted that he does not need to communicate. He keeps himself to himself in the Divine Silence, and Ignatius of Antioch has a familiar line about what a great thing silence is in a bishop.[14] First you were a substance, silent and self-sufficient; and your going out into self-giving and communication was secondary and even gratuitous. Thus the One was first and its Logos came second. From this metaphysical background there arose, within the Christian as in other religious traditions, a tendency to privilege Silence, stillness, self-sufficiency and contemplation. Silence was thought to be an eloquent assertion of power and holiness. An integral substance could afford to be silent.[15] So a person in reserve is more religious than the same person in expression.

We reject this metaphysics of Silence outright. In orthodox Christianity the Word was eventually made consubstantial and coeternal with the Father, and St John's Gospel says that in the beginning was the Logos. We take this further: we say that substance does not come first, silence and self-sufficiency do not come first. Communication comes first, the endless self-unfolding motion of meaning comes first, and relations precede substances. Only the dead are silent, awesome and self-sufficient. There will be time enough for silence when I am in the grave: till then I shall communicate non-stop. Holiness is garrulity is humanity is communication is the Logos. Saints are gossips, talk is life. It is not holy to recollect yourself and keep yourself to yourself in silence. You should dissipate yourself, going out continually into language. There is of course a rhetorical use for silence within language; but the notion of silence as a specially important and religiously-valuable region outside language and ontologically prior to it can now be seen to be a mistake, just another form of death wish. The most frivolous gossip is holier, wiser and deeper than silence. Socrates, the Buddha and Jesus are all remembered as chiefly *talkers*.

Just about everything needs to be turned the other way round. We must put speech before silence, weakness before strength, self-giving before self-possession, relations before substances, dispersal before recollection, meaning before being. Carry all these reversals through and a language-theology, postmodern, dispersed and endlessly, fruitfully conversational may be found emerging from a modern reading of the New Testament.

What so far inhibits the development of a holy-communion theology is theological realism, the religion of the ego, big, self-sufficient, strong, silent, all-powerful and controlling. But how can a religion based on dying with Christ and on the pentecostal gift of tongues to the Dispersion be reconciled with continuing attachment to the Great I Am of theological realism?

(e) *Ethics and the imagination*

The fabulous complexity and variety of the world's religions, cultures and languages is evidence enough that we human beings are artists and mythmakers. We have a seemingly unstoppable productivity in generating stories and symbols, meanings and values. What is more, it seems that we always have lived and can only live within imaginary worlds of our own creation. The human animal is the animal that can live only in a dream. These imaginary worlds of ours are always in a broad sense linguistic. They involve not only the natural language and all that it conjures up but also a great deal of paralinguistic activity, namely the vast range of our symbolic behaviours, some of them traditionally-prescribed and others spontaneous. There seems to be no upper limit to the number and variety of possible cultural worlds, and everybody lives in at least one of them.

In view of all this, it may seem at first sight strange that monotheistic religion in particular should so vehemently deny to us the very powers of which its own existence is such striking evidence. In monotheistic religion all our creative world-making powers are taken from us and ascribed exclusively to God. In the traditional theology of the church before the Enlightenment, history was moulded only by God and not by human action. In socially-approved idioms people represented themselves as having been given life and nurture by God, rather than by sexual reproduction and human parent-care. God possessed all creativity, all control over meanings and values, and all cosmos-ordering power. The major religious rituals and social institutions had all originally been divinely ordained. God ruled all life. Everything was ascribed to and centred in God in a way that left us human beings sinful, impotent, unstable and in need of strong government and guidance. We could not do anything properly unless God enlightened our minds by his Spirit and strengthened our wills by his Grace. We Westerners have sometimes been amused and piqued by exotic cultural systems which appear to disclaim any causal connection between sexual intercourse and pregnancy.[16] How, we wonder, can they have wanted to deny something so *obvious*? But we have failed to recognize that in our own culture religion for its own purposes has led us similarly to deny the obvious on a truly gargantuan scale.

Why then was this? Clearly, because religion is about social control. Monotheism – Christian, and perhaps even more, Islamic – is a magnificent instrument of social control, the best there has ever been, able to discipline and unite a miscellany of warlike tribes spreading over vast territories, and make of them great civilizations. But the trick will only work if religion rigorously represses the memory of its own origins. It must make utterly unthinkable the thought that we could have evolved it all ourselves.

So, in the past at least, religion was forced to deny its own parenthood. We human beings need a common language-of-life. We need a shared and publicly authoritative order of values and meanings, we need acknowledged rituals, a kinship-system and a social order. Slowly we evolve all these things together – and then religion draws the necessary veil of oblivion over what we have made. The whole content of religion is now declared to be from Above, awesome, majestic, primal, superhuman and sacrosanct. In this way the thousand-year history of purely human and occasional writing, conflict, editing and so forth out of which the Bible emerged is somehow forgotten, and the Holy Book becomes the inerrant and authoritative Word of God. Doctrinal statements which were once the topic of very fierce and historically-specific controversies somehow get turned into immoveable cosmic fixtures. Once they were utterly questionable; now it is forbidden to question them. In right-wing religion especially, that is, religion concerned with authority and the preservation of all standards, the reason why God so completely arrogates to himself all goodness, creativity and power, and so completely monopolizes the initiative, is that it is his job to safeguard civilization by concealing the human creation of religion. God takes away from us the power to think we could have done the forbidden thing. Right-wing religion helps God by being anti-critical, anti-historical and keen on repression. Civilization depends upon the publicly-acknowledged authority of enduring standards in grammar, morality, epistemology and so forth. We must not know that we ourselves set them up and can alter them. Thus civilization rests upon a small but necessary area of forgetfulness, and that is what God guards.

In the past this concealed area was so effectively guarded that almost nobody was even aware of its existence. It was the tain of the mirror, to borrow a phrase. Everything can be seen in the mirror – except of course the silvering on the back that alone makes it possible to see everything in the mirror. The tain is wonderfully invisible, and the resulting position is one of peculiarly tormenting irony. Both for the Christian platonist

Augustine and for me it is indeed the case that in God's light we see all things. Augustine's text is beautiful, and very highly conscious. Yes, I admit it, he sees everything and he misses nothing. I enter, share and love the completeness, the strength and the clarity of his world. For him the invisible tain that makes all this reflective perspicuity possible is God. For me what makes it possible is the invisible act of repression by which the merely-human, historically-evolved and contingent character of all our thought-standards is concealed from us. For both of us the tain really does work and is quite hidden. For Augustine the invisible God makes visible everything other than himself, whereas for me God in Augustine's text, yes, really *does* make visible everything other than himself, but does it by standing in front of and concealing an act of repression. And there's no denying it, the results are terrific. Torment. For me it is we ourselves who over the millennia have slowly evolved all the norms that guide our life, and have built them into our language. Standards, customs, meanings, values, the world-order, selfhood – everything grew this way, and it is all of it purely contingent. None of it is objectively sacrosanct. We made it all.

The norms owe their authority to custom, to our acknowledgment of them, to a few frail myths, and most of all to that last vital thin layer of unconsciousness spread over everything. The truly frightful irony is that that layer of unconsciousness has an effect like dipping dry pebbles into sea-water: everything suddenly becomes so much more shiny, clear, *real* and beautiful. It is God who brings about this marvellous effect of reality, Augustine would say, and who am I to gainsay him? He's right; God is indeed the tain of the mirror that makes everything so clear, and I believe in God as Augustine does. Like him I am a Christian priest. His faith is mine. But, but, living in a period of double reflection when we have found a way of thinking the tain, though I believe in God, I believe in an historically-evolving, human and culturally-established God. I can't objectify him in the old way any more, for that would be to make him into an idol. Living in a period of super-rapid change I have watched God evolving, I have seen it all happen, and I recognize that we have now become responsible for our God. We've got to appraise him, update him, rewrite him continually. We cannot any longer just enjoy the clear vision as Augustine does; we have also to keep in good repair the hidden machinery by which the vision is obtained. For us with our forbidden knowledge nothing can ever again be quite as magically *real* as it was for Augustine, alas, for we know how the trick was done and have become responsible for what goes on behind the scenes. So for me Augustine's own kind of unconsciousness is unfortunately not possible, and the new world-wide reversion to neo-conservative religion is a willed unconsciousness that is doubly impossible. By a truly horrible paradox, it is a deliberate sin against the light in order to regain the old innocence. We cannot envy people who do that to themselves.

The beginnings of our modern dilemma may be traced back to the Italian Renaissance and its celebration of human energy and creativity. From the first it was clear that this movement had serious implications for religion. Some of the divine attributes were going at least partly to be returned into the human being, and religion would thereby be demythologized. This was an intoxicating thought, and potentially dangerous. A fascinating intermediate solution was found: the artists and writers could revive, and could exercise their new powers upon, the old Graeco-Roman literary and mythological tradition. The heathen divinities could safely be unmasked, shown to be projections, resolved back down into their human basis, manipulated and transformed in all manner of ways, and all without in any way appearing to threaten Christian truth. Indeed it was rather confirmed, as heathen religion (*scil.*, unlike Christian) was shown to be a product of the human imagination. Graeco-Roman mythological subjects also provided a vocabulary and a pretext for exploring the passions, the body, sexuality and other topics which had been more or less proscribed in Christendom. Once the creative human imagination was let loose in this world of humanized divinity, all manner of new possibilities – heroic, sensual, tender and tragic – were opened up. A life-affirming humanist ethic became a tangible possibility. Something of its mood and method of treatment inevitably spread across into the way Christian subjects were handled, but for three centuries and more a veil was kept in place between heathen fables and Christian truth. During this entire period you could not say or think openly that Christian religious objects and doctrinal themes had the same standing in relation to human psychology, the human imagination and human creativity as had pagan objects and themes. Thus for a substantial period the early modern mind trained itself and sharpened its tools by practising only on pagan materials, in preparation for the really serious business of trying to turn back and understand its own religion.

The resulting struggle was titanic, but at some point the Western mind saw the tain, in the sense I am here talking about. It ended the faith of the first who saw it – Bruno Bauer, Strauss, Feuerbach, shall we say? – but Kierkegaard, I think, saw it and yet believed. Some others since have seen it, but I have paid them my tribute elsewhere. Our present concern is with the aftermath.

For the drift of our argument has become clear. The classic Christian thinkers usually maintained that 'the world' (i.e., civil society) was pretty bad and that unregenerate human nature was pretty bad too. Both would stay much the same until the end of the world. The city of man was irreformable, and human nature was a more or less fixed essence. Thus Augustine's pronouncements on major social questions seem designed to head off social protest by persuading us that various major social evils are just permanent facts of the human condition. There will always be war, persecution, prostitution – that is human nature. You cannot abolish such things.

We differ from Augustine in that we have social sciences and two or three centuries of experience of planned social reform. We have at least some ideas about how societies work, and some quantitative evidence – public health and life-expectancy figures, for example – to prove that the conditions of human life genuinely can be made better. The modern state has thus become responsible for the conditions of life of its citizens in a way that did not apply before the Enlightenment. Conditions that Augustine portrayed as facts of nature out of our control are now seen as cultural facts that can be changed.

By the same token, we now know a lot more about what religious ideologies are and how they work. We can no longer represent religious objects, truths, values, institutions and the like as unalterable super-human verities. They are cultural. We made them; we are responsible for reforming and redesigning them. If, for example, architects and planners can design out the violence from housing estates, as they now talk of doing, then the Pope can design out the antisemitism from Christian doctrine and liturgy (as he has partly or largely done already) and he can design out

the male supremacist bias from Christian symbolism and institutions (as he is going to have to do). Hollywood designed out
the racism from Western pictures long ago, and injuns no longer
bite the dust. *It is possible to correct our myths.* So what I am
asking for in Christian theology and ethics is no more than what
is already known to be possible, and is beginning to happen. We
need an explosion of the imagination to give us the courage and
the freedom to treat our own deep doctrinal and evaluative
assumptions somewhat as the Renaissance artists treated pagan
mythology. We must take a thoroughly naturalistic view of our
own faith, fully recognizing its expressive human ethical and
emotional meaning, and designing out the power-hungry, life-
hating, psychologically perverse and repressive elements in the
tradition we have received. The days when a Christian theologian
or moralist could be a respectable person, a hack, a defender of
the *status quo*, someone who sets out to vindicate the faith and
the ethic just as they stand – those days are clearly over. The task
of the critical theologian and moralist is to put up a redevelopment proposal, a scheme for reform.

Of the general rubric 'Raise values!' – that is, avoid the
negative and reactive, and concentrate on affirmation – I have
written something elsewhere. Here we need to add something
about an appropriate future *pratique de soi*, or manner of shap-
ing oneself and one's life. If there is no question of measuring oneself up against any external or transcendent norms, then we
would seem to be reduced to an aesthetics of existence: one
should seek to live a religiously beautiful life. But I am not quite
saying that. One should live a dedicated life, a religious life, a life
of other-directed attention and care which seeks to bestow value
upon and to enhance the public estimation of whatever it is to
which one devotes one's life. But it is easy to think of moving and
exemplary religious lives which were not *beautiful*, so much as
fated, tragic, destined, selflessly devoted, grotesque, futile, clown-
ish, heroic and so on. All are valid. Religion should encompass
not just one but every face of our human lot – and it has many
faces. And whereas the dandy is a person of artifice determined
fully to control his life, many of the religious life-outcomes I
have described are not chosen, and cannot really be chosen.
Nelson appears to have *planned* his own apotheosis as a national
hero, for example by asking that his body be taken home so that

he could expect a State funeral on the Thames. But a religious person does not attempt to make a public artefact of herself as the dandy and Nelson did. A religious person casts herself into life, lives hard and accepts what befalls her. She loves to be creative, but does not seek self-iconization. A religious person does have a life-project, but does not have an *ambition* to be achieved come what may. Rather, what makes her religious is that she is receptive enough to allow her interaction with life continuously to modify her project. So life becomes something between a quest and a pilgrimage: certainly we move towards a goal, but the way we conceive the goal and what we count as being movement towards it undergoes constant change. What makes our life a spiritual life is not so much that *we* are changing or that we are progressively achieving our goals, as rather that our interaction with life is itself a religious education, changing our beliefs, our desires and ideals even as we pursue them.

4

...IS UNACCEPTABLE TO THE CHURCH

(a) Truth, power and social cohesion

The dilemma is clear now. The conception of faith and of the religious life to which we have been led is as demythologized, as plural and as freelance as can well be imagined. The postmodern believer has got to be like the postmodern artist, constantly reinventing herself and centrifugal in the straightforward sense of fleeing from all stable Centres, scattering. At an End-time, when centres and strongholds break down, one must take to the hills. In any case, postmoderns *like* to be protean, mistrusting selfsameness and strong identity and preferring plurality and difference. They don't really want to become locked into fixed positions, routines, identities and allegiances. They prefer to be a little shifty and evasive, keeping the freedom to move. They do not deplore, indeed they rather relish the fact that we do not have Jesus himself but only four different portraits of him. That is how it has to be. There never *was* any real-Jesus-himself, but only a plurality of images, reactions and relationships. There isn't any real me either, only a plurality of *personae*, roles, relations and reactions. There is no final truth about me that will one day emerge and put an end to the present diversity of opinions about me. I am going to remain disputed and insubstantial. Nor can I regret this. If disappearing into plurality was good enough for God in becoming incarnate, then it ought to be good enough for me. So God has dispersed himself and the self should be dispersed also.

The church, however, is *not* going to disperse itself. The times may call faith to be centrifugal, but the church will continue to be centripetal. An enduring historical institution with a powerful professional officer-class cannot but be in favour of continuity with tradition, unity, selfsameness, distinctiveness, discipline, stability and good order. It *must* believe in one church, one faith, one Lord; it *must* see truth, power and legitimacy as coming down through its upper ranks from Above. We will make no progress by urging the facts of cultural change and statistical decline as reasons why the church must modernize herself or perish. The problem is that the kind of modernization that is called for is tantamount to institutional suicide. The fragmentation and ferment it would bring must spell dissolution; and institutions simply do not let themselves go in that way. They hang on.

There was once a time, a millennium and more ago, when the Patriarch of Constantinople was a bigger fellow than the Pope of Rome. Now he has fewer souls living within and subject to his jurisdiction than the average town parish priest in Western Europe. But of course the Patriarch's claims and pretensions are not one whit diminished, and it would be absurd to press him to face facts and adapt himself to his reduced circumstances. He's not going to do that. Similarly, there has been in the Western church during the past half century much enthusiasm for 'the theology of the laity'.[1] But it is quite certain that the laity will be upgraded in the church only so far as the process does not diminish the traditional powers and prerogatives of the clergy. The clergy will not surrender any of the monopoly control over doctrine, over most of the sacraments, over church government and so forth, which they have enjoyed since early times. Anything that makes lay folk feel good and perhaps even increases their numbers is naturally to be welcomed. But so far as the people who control it are concerned the church is about one thing only, spiritual power, and power is never surrendered voluntarily. And since the church's power is sealed in and by her dogmatic definitions, she can never voluntarily disown them. Nor will reasoning make any headway against them. Rationality is not the issue.

A truth which the church does her best to keep hidden, but which is of great importance for understanding these matters, is that since very early times there have been two Christianities, one for the clergy and one for the laity. For the priest, who is a stipendiary professional, the church is a centred/concentrated power structure and he is one of the power elite. He gets his place in the scheme of things and his feeling of life from being a channel of spiritual power. By contrast the layperson, being powerless in the church, has a religion of love, reconciliation, and reliance for strength upon God and the fortifying ministrations of his church. There are a very few laypeople who adopt something of the values and outlook of the clergy and can even get to have a sort of secondary participation in their power. They may include certain lawyers, employees of the church and its organizations, elected representatives, committee people, a few musicians and writers and such like. These ecclesiastical laypeople stand in the same sort of relation to the clergy as Warrant Officers bear to the officer class in the Army, but they are generally thought to be slightly absurd and anomalous. Really, we feel, laypeople and clerics *ought* to have different religions. The cleric should be interested in the church, its growth, the truth of its doctrines, its power, his career, the gossip, whereas in a layperson such concerns are out of place. She should be interested in culture, in ethics and in the imaginative side of religion – that is, the capacity of its symbolism and its vision to irradiate and transfigure life.

Thus the distinction between the clergy and the laity seals in the church a distinction between two different Christianities, a Christianity of strength and spiritual power and a Christianity of needy, powerless love and forgiveness, which have coexisted in the church since the days of the Apostles. It is not difficult to think of large numbers of stories told in the church whose function is to conceal the conflict between the two Christianities by describing friendly encounters between typical exponents of each of them. The meeting of Francis of Assisi with Pope Innocent III is a case in point. Many writers, however, have chosen rather to stress the contrast between the two religions. Dostoyevsky uses a fictional encounter story in which he has Christ meeting the Grand Inquisitor to highlight the issues. Tolstoy was equally hostile to sacerdotalism. A recent English writer, Graham Shaw, has interestingly analysed the co-existence of the two religions in the Pauline letters.[2] Obviously influenced by Tolstoy, he regards the love of wielding spiritual power over human souls as pathological.

By contrast, Nietzsche's verdict on both Christianities is ambiguous. His mixed feelings about the original gospel of Jesus himself are well-known, and so is his hostility to the priestly type as exemplified by Paul, with his doctrines of sin and its expiation. But Nietzsche, like Kierkegaard, refused to give Martin Luther unqualified praise for having broken the power of the church in Northern Europe. On the contrary, Luther lowered our standards. He bequeathed to us a certain 'plebeianism of the spirit':

> 'Modern ideas' also belong to this peasant rebellion of the north against the colder, more ambiguous and mistrustful spirit of the south that built its greatest monument in the Christian church. Let us not forget in the end what a church is, as opposed to any 'state'. A church is above all a structure for ruling that secures the highest rank for the *more spiritual* human beings and that *believes* in the power of spirituality to the extent of forbidding itself the use of all the cruder instruments of force; and on this score alone the church is under all circumstances a *nobler* institution than the state.[3]

That is notably generous: Nietzsche is willing to salute a disciplined aristocracy of the spirit even when it wears priestly robes. And he is right to criticize the Christianity of powerless introvertive bliss ('the kingdom of God is within you') as schizoid. One cannot bear to be touched, one recoils from conflict.[4] That's wrong. So we conclude that the disorder in Christianity arises, in part at least, from the divorce between the two religions. Spiritual power is too much concentrated and objectified in the male clergy with their orthodoxy, their franchise on forgiveness, their chain of command and their proper channels of Grace. A Pentecost-Christianity does not repudiate spiritual power, but it does seek to distribute it more evenly so that each layperson gains the courage to be creative and to be *different*. Difference is the real challenge: it is easy to be the same as others, one sheep in the flock, but hard to be different and to tolerate difference. Besides, existing structures are entirely directed towards imposing sameness. To ask for difference is in effect to call for an end to the division of the church into shepherds and sheep. But as things stand we are deeply habituated to the distinction, and do not want to give it up. The shepherds, that is the clergy, need the supernatural realm as the source of their power; and the sheep, that is the laity, need the supernatural realm as a source of consolations for their weakness. In order to become mature in Christ both parties have got to grow up and renounce the supernatural world, and with it their inequality to each other. They have to see that the chief social function of the supernatural world is the creation and maintenance of certain power-relations. But this they don't wish to see. The hierarchs do not wish to give up their power and the laity do not wish to give up their weakness, and it is hard to tell which need, the need for power or the need for weakness, is the greater.

This example reminds us of how deeply supernatural belief has entered into our psychology and institutions, and still robs us of our creativity. Supernaturalism induces passivity in relation to a divinely-established order. Its influence shows in the language of penitence, the joining of hands in prayer, the downcast eyes, the hushed and deferential atmosphere, the rhetoric of weakness and power, and the bottom-of-the-cosmic-pecking-order body postures that we still associate with 'church'.

It is all untruth. We still have a myth that morality is to conform our behaviour to timeless and superhuman norms, whereas just history, just the passage of time, makes it entirely obvious that morality is cultural and we are ourselves making it all the while. We human beings in our daily interaction are constantly pioneering new values, new objects of moral concern and new forms of life. We make our values all the time, just as we make language and culture all the time. That is how things are now, but we do not seem to want to know. We want to keep up the old habit of using our religion as a way of denying our creativity, rather than as the principal field in which to exercise it. And this is absurdly out of place now. Somewhere between one and two centuries ago, the mass of people in the advanced countries suddenly emerged from under the mighty Shadows beneath which they had always hitherto lived. They came out into the sunlight. Amazing. The change shows very clearly in art. Until the early nineteenth century and with only rather limited exceptions, high art had mostly been about glory. It had been monumental, public, allegorical, mythological, and almost always in one way or another ideological. It advertised the power of various mighty figures and themes, noble, royal, civic, religious and so forth. It was these figures whose greatness had hitherto overshadowed all human life. In relation to them ordinary people were low life, servants, cannon fodder, somewhat comical, unimportant and expendable. Ordinary people were not quite as real as their betters; you did not need to trouble yourself to remember their names.

Yet in *plein air* Impressionist painting these people suddenly come out into the sunshine. The Powers have vanished. This painting is extraordinarily unideological and accessible to us. There is about as little propaganda, religious, political or moral, as one could well imagine. The message is that there doesn't need to be a message any longer. The Shadows have fled: the sun has come out.

Against this background what are we to make of Christians' continuing, anachronistic attachment to supernaturalism? Inertia, reluctance to adjust to what has happened and sheer nostalgia for the musty, overshadowed and fear-ridden past all no doubt play their part. But for our spiritual backwardness a price must be paid. The church slithers rapidly downhill intellectually. Supernatural belief becomes more softheaded year by year. The idioms in which Christians speak of God's action, life after death, grace, the ministry of healing, intercessory prayer, evil spirits and 'deliverance', the work of the Holy Spirit, the will of God and the rest – all the popular currency of supernatural belief – becomes daily more slack, sorry and shapeless. The language has already become so debased, far beyond any possibility of revival, that many of us, although we are and will remain determined Christians, simply cannot bring ourselves to use it. I just cannot get my tongue round those ways of speaking. Even if they were in better shape they would still be objectionable because they would devalorize their secular neighbours. Thus the language in which the church talks about her special supplementary sacramental 'ministry of healing' is a shambles, but even if it were more orderly and could be used in good conscience, it would still be objectionable, because insofar as it won credibility it would devalue the intellectually and morally more sober work done by the practitioners of decent scientific medicine. Similarly, exorcism and the 'ministry of deliverance' is a mess; but even if it were not a mess it would still be objectionable because then it would relatively devalorize the honourable work done by psychiatrists and psychotherapists.

In cases such as these the attempt of the church to keep a marginal supernaturalism going cannot hope to rise to anything more than fringe status; yet nor can we wish it were doing any better, because that would make the overall outcome still worse. In our own human, historical and science-based world, supernaturalism cannot decently be allowed to become more than a tolerated superstition. The language that is used is sufficient evidence of this. And not even the most traditional Christian really wishes things were otherwise, for any side-by-side coexistence of the supernatural and the natural has ethically unendurable implications. Suppose you have two sisters, one a dedicated doctor and the other a faith-healer, and suppose that the evidence that the faith-healer really is being used by God and really is performing supernatural miracles of healing grows stronger and stronger. Well, the stronger it gets the more the straight doctor's dedicated work becomes a second-best, 'merely' human and secular, and so is robbed of religious dignity. We cannot possibly want that. So we ought to have the courage to admit that if there is ever to be a serious modern Christianity it must repudiate supernaturalism as intellectually and morally undesirable – yes, and even *religiously* undesirable, too.

But how is the church to adjust to all this? It is evident that while postmodernist ideas about language and meaning in many ways increase the interest and attractiveness of religious language and symbolism, by the same token they make the position of any confessional society more difficult. How can the church function in a postmodern era? One obvious possibility is that the church may cease to be a divine society and instead become more of a theatrical costumier, a rich treasury of fascinating old idioms, practices, symbols and suchlike that people rummage through, freely borrowing whatever they can make use of in their own lives. This is of course by no means a new way of treating religion. The traditional faiths of China and India do not have a congregation, a *laos* or people-of-the-Book which is a law-governed religious society distinct from the surrounding civil society. Rather, the great Temples and other sanctuaries are simply available to all as ritual centres, places of resort and cultural strongholds. People flock to them and make varied use of them, but there is no unified and disciplined *plebs sancta Dei* in the sense familiar in the Abrahamic faiths.

Now many people in Christian cultures are already visiting their own churches and monasteries in a Hindu rather than an ecclesiastical spirit. The regular liturgical worship of the church presupposes a clearly defined and highly committed community. But most visitors to cathedrals are not nowadays members of such a community, nor do they wish to be. They prefer to be freelance pilgrims and holy tourists. Churchpeople look down on this, but the tourist may well be a person who loves Christian culture and is appropriating something of it in her own way, in order to build it into the myth, the morality and the project of her own life. What is the objection? Often, ecclesiastical Christians describe this freelance Christianity as being 'folk-religion', with a suggestion that it is undisciplined, unauthorized and therefore of low value. But such an attitude merely betrays the extent to which ecclesiastical Christianity is still authoritarian, and confirms the opinion of those who suspect that the only genuinely free church is the invisible church of the freelance Christians. Alternatively, if (like me) you still feel strongly the social and political importance of the church as a divine society and a guardian of alternative values, you need to show how there can be such a society without the usual authoritarianism and hostility to dissenters.

We have been suggesting that an authentic postmodern Christianity must be highly plural, freelance, 'feminine', multifarious and centrifugal, preferring dispersal and difference. Historically postmodernism is heavily indebted to the Hegel-Nietzsche-Heidegger critique of Platonism and 'onto-theo-logy', which has shown up the way Western thought has always tended to privilege unity, selfsameness, presence, timelessness, necessity and Logos. This set of deep assumptions was discovered as people strove to break out of the world-view that they had generated. However, one unlooked-for consequence is that we can now look back at Augustinian Christianity with new concepts that enable us to appreciate more clearly than before what a prodigiously powerful and coherent system of thought it was, *and why*. Postmodernism must be plural enough to allow one to choose against it, and Alasdair MacIntyre, for example, has therefore recently announced his return to Augustinian Christianity.[5]

The very fact that such a return is a genuinely available option once more gives much encouragement to those who argue that the church need neither reform herself nor abandon her historic faith. However, there are dangers. MacIntyre must be aware that Augustinianism is subtly transformed by the newly knowing spirit in which one returns to it. When we have understood the nature of the strength that we are choosing to go back to, we do not quite return to the old innocence. One knows and has bought in advance, for example, the implications of Augustinianism for social ethics – which makes a knowing return to it politically very questionable, in my view at least.

A third possible relation between the church and postmodernism is this: we may stay within the church but work to loosen it up. We cannot hope, for reasons already given, to reform doctrine directly, but we may be able somewhat to relax the grip of the authoritarian psychology by campaigning for the marriage of the clergy, the admission of women to the priesthood, the rights of the laity, liberalization of discipline and moral teachings, modernization of worship and so forth. Arguing on behalf of the ordination of women, for example, has a cunningly subversive effect. We play the game by innocently appealing to those elements in the tradition that affirm the equality of the sexes, and thereby expose those other strands in the tradition which deny the equality of the sexes. This forces into the open things which the authorities do not want to have brought out into the open, and by setting the tradition against itself undermines its claims to unchanging unity and authority. The powers that be are put on the spot: they certainly don't want to have to admit that much of existing religious ideology functions to maintain the subjection of women. Politically, they are compelled to say with as much grace as they can muster that of course they accept the feminist case, and of course they cannot think of any sound theological objections to the ordination of women to the priesthood. Only, it's not convenient to change things just now. It would be a departure from tradition, or bad for ecumenical relations or something. But in fact the authorities know very well that from their point of view there are conclusive theological objections to the ordination of women, because existing doctrine is and was designed to be highly sexist, and if they yield on this point then Christianity must eventually be transformed. So they feel very uncomfortable.

Our present argument has suggested that under present conditions there is no chance of bringing about the renewal and modernization of the Christian church by a direct assault. But with the help of just a little low cunning the postmodern believer within the church can find cracks in the Rock and insert wedges.

Another example: Western church leaders profess themselves strongly in favour of freedom of religious worship and expression in the communist countries. We should echo their sentiments enthusiastically, adding mildly that it would be wonderful if there were more tolerance and freedom of religious worship and expression within our churches, too. In general, the keener the church becomes on human rights, the more encouragment it gives to those of us who would like to see just a little more respect for human differences, human rights and human worth built into the church's own doctrines and structures.

In these ways then we *can* after all help history along a bit. We cannot win by a direct assault, and there is no discernible likelihood that the historic mainline churches will voluntarily set about renewing themselves. But by relating present-day issues to conflicts within the received tradition, we can help to demythologize and destabilize authority and to liberate religious psychology. That is a very positive and constructive thing to do.

(b) *Postmodernism and the question of God*

Postmodernism[6] is a cultural condition in which there isn't much 'reality' around. Alternatively, we may say that the line between the real and the fictional has become very blurred. It is easy to describe how this has happened. Since the late-seventeenth-century Anglo-Saxon culture has sought to maintain a clear distinction between science and the arts, between a highly descriptive and disciplined sort of language used for reporting facts just as they are, undistorted, uninterpreted and without comment, and a very different, flighty, emotive, metaphorical kind of language in which people imaginatively transform the world and dream their dreams. Po-faced and well-drilled, the scientists label things one by one and copy the structure of the objective world. That's reality. But hard facts are hard work, and people need to let their hair down and relax. The arts are there to help us unwind, and the typical practitioner should be like Dylan Thomas, the exact opposite of a serious scientist, and therefore a wild, undisciplined, hopelessly subjective and irrational alcoholic *wunderkind*. That's unwound for you, that's *really* unwound.

The whole scheme depends upon our ability to define and justify the initial separation of the rational-literal from the emotional-metaphorical uses of language, the literal use of language being associated with reality, truth and discipline, and the metaphorical use of language being linked with fantasy and the expression of the emotions. The literal is described as hard, dry, objective and self-controlled (i.e. masculine) whereas the metaphorical and arty is soft, wet, subjective and self-indulgent. Today, the distinction cannot help looking like a piece of applied sexism: the real, serious world belongs to men, whereas the 'soft' world of art, ideality and pleasure is the sphere of women. But difficulties with the distinction go back at least to Hume. Scepticism about the one world tends to spread to the other, as when (to put it in more recent terms) it is suggested that if in the soft world language is always metaphorical and reality is imaginatively interpreted, then perhaps the same may be true of the hard world also?

To keep this disturbing suggestion at bay and defend their own hardness, scientists need to be unaware of language. For them it is transparent. Words open directly onto concepts; concepts are or can easily be made fully determinate, and the observer has well-defined procedures for checking whether or not a certain concept is instantiated or exemplified in reality. A well-made and properly-tested body of knowledge is a diagrammatic representation of a bit of the world. It portrays objective things and their relations out there in the world in much the same way as a well-made map of London represents things and their relations in the city of London.

Until recent times religious thinkers – at least, the ones who got published – were men, keen to prove their own intellectual virility. In terms of the standard Anglo-Saxon philosophy of culture as I have described it, that meant you tried to promote religion from the soft world to the hard. Religion wasn't just a fantasy for females; it was heavy stuff, real knowledge. The ambition to prove this determined the agenda for the philosophy of religion. You needed (1) a clear definition of God, (2) a rigorous investigation of the validity of the arguments for the existence of God, (3) an account of how our ordinary vocabulary may be stretched a little so it can be used to make genuinely factual assertions about God, (4) an account of how statements about God can be verified, or at least confirmed or disconfirmed, and (5), as an appendix or perhaps at an earlier stage in the proceedings, you needed also to find solutions to the various paradoxes that talk of God as omnipotent and omniscient generates.

After these preliminaries you could go on to discuss the relations between God and the world: his providence, the problem of evil, revelation, miracle, prayer, and the origin and destiny of humankind.

The syllabus aimed to bring the whole question of God as close to the early-modern ideal of scientific knowledge as could be achieved. And it was the assumptions behind the programme, not the execution of the programme, which decided what sort of God was going to be discovered. He would be a real man's God, Plato's *Demiourgos*, the God of scientific theism or 'designer realism'.[7] Since the later seventeenth century this God has been the dominant God of the churches in the English-speaking world at least, and people are still striving to connect him even to modern physical cosmology.

The point to be emphasized is that this God, and the whole religious style that went with him, was tied to a certain map of culture, doctrine of language and truth, and ideal of science. The whole cluster of ideas gave us our sense of reality, or rather just *constituted reality for us*, for about three centuries. At the University of Oxford, where the traditional battle by the Anglo-Saxons to keep out the French Revolution and German idealist philosophy and to prolong the world-view of the seventeenth and eighteenth centuries is still being fought as courageously as ever, Professor Richard Swinburne maintains the whole cycle of Cartesian-empiricist doctrine intact.[8] He is fighting for 'reality', *his* reality, reality as he sees it. This 'reality' of his is, as I have been suggesting, a magical effect produced by a certain set of doctrines about God, culture, language, truth and science. The doctrines elaborate a few sexist metaphors and binary oppositions (only, you are not allowed to know this) and represent the ideology of the masculine intellectual-religious-political Establishment around 1660–1700. The Bishops, the Royal Society, the Glorious Revolution, Free Trade, the experimental philosophy. So this 'reality' is a human cultural product with a certain date and a certain political situation written all over it (only you are not allowed to be aware of this). Philosophy is a special kind of deceit whereby ideas that are in fact occasional and political productions are projected out upon the cosmos and made to seem natural and inevitable, part of the perennial constitution of things. In this way a 'reality' is constructed. Intellectually, precritical or pre-Nietzschean philosophy works in just the same way as fundamentalist religion. It represses the memory of the highly-specific and occasional origins of the ideas it trades in. Secondly, it represses awareness of the political motivation of that first act of repression. It then represents itself as being apolitical and timeless, independent of history, culture and group interests. This makes it very useful, precisely *politically*, and its ideas develop into a 'reality' that people come to take for granted. Eventually they cling to it and fight tenaciously for it. For them it *is* reality, the masculine God's reality, the hard stuff, science.

The connection between truth and reality on the one hand, and certain claims to social privilege on the other, is nowhere more clear than in this case of scientific realism. The claim to possess the one-and-only method for gaining objective knowledge of the real world out there functions to justify the claim to a certain social status and level of public funding for research. Anyone who appears to undermine the philosophy of scientific realism therefore encounters a special kind of *anger*, and does so not just because he threatens to undermine the claims of the scientific community to social status and public funding, but also and more deeply because he threatens to demythologize the scientists' sense of reality, by exposing the little devices of concealment and mythicization by which it is generated. These people aren't hypocrites; their faith in their own propaganda is vitally important to them.

A tell-tale sign of this is the way the philosophy of science is bracketed with the history of science – and the scientists cordially dislike *both*. I don't want to know about the history of science because, by reminding me of the culturally conditioned character of scientific knowledge and of the sheer rate at which what passes for knowledge changes, it demythologizes the ideological claim of present-day scientific knowledge to be a more-or-less permanently reliable picture of a permanent objective world. So there are excellent reasons why the scientists should resent being asked to spend valuable time thinking about the history of their own subject and the philosophical questions it raises.

I am suggesting then that the specialist student of the history and philosophy of science is perceived as a political threat, and calls down upon her or his own head a special deep *anger* on the part of the scientists, because she threatens to uncover the little acts of concealment and mythicization that make possible the scientists' self-confidence and power, their concern for truth and their sense of reality. Who wants to know about the little deeply-buried lies that make truth possible? In particular, who wants to know that the thing we most crave – a sense of reality – is a special kind of illusion? It is a bit of ideology hiding a little concealment which in turn hides a bit of sexism. I'm a big boy, I've got a hard fact.

Thus the *anger* I am talking about protects a terrible secret that it would destroy most people to learn. And our discussion has already suggested that a similar anger protects against historical criticism the objectivist illusions on which conservative religion rests, and the errors about truth and reality on which precritical philosophy rests. The wrath of God is the believer's own anger against his own doubt when he hears it voiced by the heretic. The conservative religious believer does not want to know that the scriptures, our religious beliefs and values and practices, our symbols and our forms of religious experience, all have a purely human history. So this obvious truth has got to be repressed, and then a fierce watchdog has to be set in front of the repression. This watchdog is [God/religious authority/pure anger] all rolled into one, and to conceal the truth that its job is to conceal truth, it is declared to be itself the glorious fulness of truth. So the conservative religious believer represses the knowledge of the history of religion, much as philosophy before Hegel, and a good deal of philosophy since Hegel, too, has repressed the knowledge of its own historical-cultural conditioning.

The first thinker fully to recognize the extent to which culture so far has been a tissue of illusions, self-deception, lies piled one upon another (and to see also how utterly stultifying, how self-refuting and how annihilating is this very recognition) was Nietzsche. Postmodernism is the cultural outcome, after early attempts to escape from nihilism have been found to fail. A whole series of classical assumptions about language have broken down. A word does not autonomously have a durable clear-and-distinct meaning: meaning is differential, it is use, it is a complex and ever-shifting thing. Truth is not one-to-one correspondence between language and reality, for nobody can take up a fully-independent standpoint and vocabulary for seeing and defining the way the two orders nestle together. What is it that fits snugly up against what, and where? And what are our knowledge-systems supposed to be, anyway? From early-modern science we have inherited the realistic idea that a well-formed human knowledge-system is a sort of participation in God's absolute knowledge of the world. What's *that*? It's control, *mastery*. God is masculine, nature is feminine. Knowledge is always linked with power, control and virility as is clearly shown by the prominence of imagery of strength and hardness in the dominant branches of knowledge. Knowledge is potency, is power. It is to *master* one's *subject*.

But there is worse to come. Polarizing man and woman, culture develops around a number of contrasts: hard-soft, literal-metaphorical, primary-secondary, real-fictitious, disciplined-indulgent, descriptive-expressive and so on. Woman is soft, plural, metaphorical, emotional, evasive, secondary and fickle, whereas man is hard, singular, literal, rational, direct and primary. I'm suggesting that all these contrasts are related. When one of them collapses, it tends to cause others to collapse as well. And of all the contrasts, perhaps the one whose breakdown causes ripples to spread most widely is the fact-interpretation contrast which declares that man is a straight fact, whereas woman is devious, disputable, an interpretation.[9] For since Kant we have increasingly recognized that interpretation goes all the way down, that is, that the very first stage of our apprehension of anything already involves the application of a concept to it and therefore is already an interpretation of it. Concepts are meanings, meanings are vested in languages, there are many different languages, and languages change. From this it follows that Descartes and the empiricists were wrong; there isn't any infallible and incorrigible apprehension of the sheerly-given. Eve has got there first. Into our very first apprehension of anything there already enters something interpretative, disputable, plural and female. Do we need to remind ourselves that etymologically a fact is a fiction, something *made*, something which therefore might have been made a bit differently because we might have got hold of it in a slightly different manner?

In Kantian terms, objects must conform to our concepts, that is, the only world we can know is a world that we ourselves have formed. As Kant puts it:

> Experience is itself a species of knowledge which involves understanding, and understanding has rules which I must presuppose as being in me prior to objects being given to me, and therefore as being *a priori*. They find expression in *a priori* concepts to which all objects of experience necessarily conform, and with which they must agree.[10]

Kant is right to say that I can know the world only by putting a construction upon it, that is, by interpreting it. He is also right to say that the interpretative grid that I must lay over experience in order to make it intelligible to myself is logically independent of and prior to the data that it makes intelligible. But he is in error when he says that the interpretative grid or order of concepts that we must use is single (in that for him there can be only *one* such grid) and is absolutely *a priori*. He was led into this error by the ideological term 'concept'. This term seems to designate a non-linguistic but determinate and even suprahuman thought-form. By using the word 'concept' instead of the word 'word', Kant avoids recognizing the dependence of all thought upon language, and therefore the historical-cultural conditioning of all thought. The word 'concept' was used by Kant and many other philosophers in order to repress or to defer the awareness of what would otherwise be obvious – namely, our linguisticality and *therefore* the interpretative and perspectival character of all knowledge. *Knowledge?* – that's another ideological term: we should say *sentences*, in order to keep our attention fixed on language. Concepts, knowledge, truth – words such as these, although they are only words, are used by philosophers as if they were more than words, as if merely to pronounce them were immediately to be ushered into a supralinguistic world of intelligible essences and absolute comprehension. In the way philosophers use terms such as concepts, knowledge, truth there is even to this day a suggestion that our thinking and our knowledge are unchallengeably authoritative because they are a participation in the absolute thought and knowledge of a masculine God.

But I am saying that in order to avoid all this ideological mystification we need to keep our attention firmly fixed on language. So we will take Kant's formula, *objects must conform to our concepts*, that is, *concepts go all the way down*, to be equivalent to *interpretation goes all the way down*, and so in turn equivalent to *language goes all the way down*. Since there is no thinking which is not couched in some kind of language, and no apprehension of the world which is not language-like, everything is filtered through language. (If perchance you dispute this thesis then, as before, kindly step forward and state your objection in some medium other than language.) And although there's no Truth, the interesting, illuminating metaphysical metaphor to which these considerations have led us is that what used to be called 'reality' was a bit of masculinist ideology; in reality, reality is as impossibly plural, fictitious and feminine as Writing. The world is like a whole shelf of novels: that is postmodernism.

Need it be said that I am not denying that the Rock of Gibraltar is 'there', or that we have many powerful sciences? Only, we used to claim for our knowledge a kind of objectivity or absolute foundedness that we can no longer claim. Postmodernism is just the belated full realization that our knowledge is just human, a function of our contingent human conventions, capacities, needs and interactions, an imaginative construction which since it is perforce wholly carried in language, cannot help but be what language is. That is all that postmodernism is – but, being that, it is more completely the death and dispersal of the old objective metaphysical God, with his masculine pronouns, than any previous philosophical movement has been.

The old Kantian style of *agnosticism*, though conceding that various propositions in metaphysical theism might be true, held that we could not determine the matter. It was beyond the limits of human thought. There was once a kind of *absolute idealism* which said that personalistic theism was true enough at its own rather popular level, but which proposed to transcend it and attain a higher truth. Then there was an old-fashioned *atheism* which, while acknowledging that beliefs about God were meaningful enough, argued that they could be shown to be false. There was also, later, a kind of *positivism* which said that religious beliefs were too vague to be meaningful. Religion fails because it regards falsifiability as impiety: that is, it won't let its own tenets ever become definite enough to be testable and therefore capable of a truth-value.

Now all these four previous great challenges to theism are of great interest, and we might spend a profitable hour or two debating how far any of them have been satisfactorily answered. But postmodernism undercuts them all. It is a linguistic dispersal of God which undercuts the whole issue by questioning the ways of thinking, the deep assumptions, distinctions and value-preferences which made it seem possible and desirable to frame the idea of God in the first place. It's not that we don't want the masculine monarch any more – no doubt we do – but we have become aware of the devices by which the desire for him was created. We don't any longer want to erect the great cosmic Arch whose keystone he was. We no longer have, and we are not attempting to recreate, the pyramidal social and cosmic order that he headed. We are uncomfortably aware of the moral dangers, the threat to human freedom and diversity, implicit in any attempt to systematize every aspect of life and the world under one absolute Authority. The painful fact is that the more objective, unified, sexist and authoritative the idea of God becomes, the more damage it does. The people who have the most realistic view of God are just the ones who are the most angry, emotionally crippled and violently prejudiced against minorities. To this day the old guilt-inducing objective God ruins lives on a vast scale, yet such is human nature that people are still queueing up to be ruined by him. They want themselves to be 'converted' to him, but still more do they want to offer their children to him – and especially their daughters. Schools designed to damage girls are ever-popular with parents.

So horrific a thing and so engrained is religious authoritarianism that many writers have thought that the word 'God' is beyond rehabilitation and should be dropped from the Christian vocabulary. However we try to reinterpret it, so long as the word remains in use it will continue to activate the archetype of the jealous, angry Father. 'God' must be forgotten, and any useful linguistic jobs the word did will have to be reassigned to other terms.

As a programme for church reform, though, Christian atheism is a non-starter. Reinterpretation it is going to have to be, but it must be a truly liberating reinterpretation that genuinely and permanently banishes the repressive old death-machine notion of God.

The starting point is obvious: Pentecost and the dogma of the Holy Trinity. The crucial point about the Trinity, which I confess I did not myself grasp until the 1980s, is just how far the full coequality and co-eternity of the Second and Third Persons is an invitation to demythologize. Hegel saw it[11] and I knew he'd seen it, so why did I not see it? I don't know: but the full coequality and coeternity of the Son means that everything the Father is, the Son is also. And when the Son completely and irrevocably commits himself to becoming human then God has become human, without remainder. So everything that God is, this fellow human being beside me now is.

Thus far, so familiar: the dogma of the *plenary* incarnation of God in Christ licenses the thoroughgoing transformation of Christianity into religious humanism. As we have long known, this much was seen with great clarity by Feuerbach and his generation. But let us continue: the Third Person of the Trinity, the Holy Spirit of God, is also coequally and coeternally God of God. So in pouring himself out as Spirit God pours himself out completely. He pours himself out into fellowship; that is, into inter-subjectivity; that is, into relationality; that is, into the movement of signs. So the God of Bethlehem is a Modern God, that is, a radical humanist God; but the God of Pentecost is a postmodern God who has ceased to be a Substance and has instead become the interrelatedness of everything, the endless movement of meaning within which we and everything else are constituted. Such is the new understanding of Spirit. The reason why in the Christian tradition the Holy Spirit has never quite gained a proper name, and has always seemed a little less distinctly individuated than the other Persons of the Trinity, is that the Holy Spirit is endlessly-moving relationality – which is what God is now. God is the medium in which we live and move and have our being, the dance of signs.

The Aristotelean God who is 'self-thinking thought' has given rise to a tradition that thinks of the divine consciousness as the autonomous self-mirroring of an absolute and immutable Substance. To be maximally self-aware, you needed to be self-sufficient, self-subsistent, autonomous, perfect, standing alone and thinking just yourself. As self-conscious, the human being was thought to be a finite, immortal spiritual substance. But I am saying that it is a mistake to equate consciousness with a certain perfection of independent substantiality. On the contrary, consciousness is relational and temporal. It exists only where there is movement, a movement from sign to sign. So we are spirit and we participate in the divine Spirit precisely because we are *not* substances. We are just a movement, a shifting pattern of relations; and so is God.

But can the church accept such ideas?

(c) *Inequalities*

A theme has emerged. In the traditional thinking that prevailed until only yesterday reality at every level was understood as being created and maintained by a primal, omnipresent and radically unequal relationship. To take the simplest example first, even where no king has been seen around for some time everyone still finds it natural to suppose that the kingdom must be held together by the common subjection of every part of it and every person within it to the monarch. That is how the child in its fairy tales assumes reality must be. That is the arrangement that seems to make sense. In the state, in the family and in the Universe, there has to be someone wearing the trousers. The presumption is that even if just at present he happens to be invisible, nevertheless he must still be about somewhere, watching over things, seeing that everything runs as it should and making small corrections as necessary.

The counterpart in philosophy of this idea of a hidden omnipresent ruling power is the ideal, intelligible order, the world of form, the world of theory and of governing rules and standards. Behind the transient particular stands the timeless unified system of rational principles and essences that makes it possible, that conditions it and explains it. Much as before, the plural and ever-changing world of phenomena is held together by the ubiquitous relation of every bit of it to the one ideal controlling order. Thus, I am just at present engaged in making spidery black marks on paper with a pen. What am I up to? I am writing English prose. In doing this, my activity continuously and at every point presupposes the whole system of the written language. That intelligible structure has to be constantly there, unchanging and invisible behind my changing activity, like God upholding the world, controlling and giving point to what I am doing. It is the transcendental presupposition of my activity. Through it and through it alone my spidery marks get meaning and can be read as words.

Versions of this motif run through the history of philosophy. For as a certain spidery mark is to the system of the written language so also physical event is to physical theory, scrap of human behaviour is to culture, and so on. Hidden systems of rules, intelligible structures, make it possible for us to construe events in our sensory apparatus as objective experience and bits of physical behaviour as moral conduct. Just like our traditional religion, science and fairy-tales, philosophy still betrays the influence of the notion that an absolute monarchy is the best model for understanding and explaining any ordered system. The system is produced by the ubiquitous action of a ruling principle throughout a domain. So we need everywhere to distinguish between rule and instance, form and matter. If the culture is successfully to establish a universe for us to live in, it has got to bang on relentlessly about a certain ubiquitous distance, dissimilarity and inequality that impinges upon everything. Everywhere there is something primary: it is a general and unchanging intelligible rule, shape or principle. Let's call it a Form. And there is also something secondary: it is a fleeting unstable material appearance or seeming that needs to be shaped and mastered. We've got to have a world, and to make a world for us the culture has got to set up these two themes in complementary apposition. One of them is an active exertion of power, and the other is a passive reception of its impress. Culture must enforce the qualitative difference between these two, and it has also got to permutate them. That is, the manner in which the ruler bears upon the ruled must be varied so as to produce physics, ethics, the social sciences and so on. This in turn means that there must also be correspondingly varied social embodiments of it in human relationships.

So it comes about that the gulf, the omnipresent radical inequality and qualitative difference that makes the world, is variously reflected in society as the gulf between man and woman, between parent and child, king and subject, claimant and official, employer and worker and so forth. To maximize its productive and creative potential the unequal relationship must be stretched to the greatest cosmic distance, permutated through various modes, and diversely embodied in human social relationships. It is very notable that the most important, symbolically-productive and society-building human ties are precisely the most unequal, those in which the greatest power is wielded. With a certain brutal realism, society has decided that mere friendship is inconsequential. To produce *reality* there must be inequality and the exercise of power.

The unequal universe reaches its logical conclusion and culmination in monotheism. God is an all-powerful Father, one who is of the older generation. Belief in him is right and proper because it comes to us, as *he* comes, from tradition, that is, from the past. The world where he dwells, the exalted, shining incorruptible world from which we derive all our standards, and by contrast with which the present age here below is always and everywhere seen as a period of decline, somehow contrives to be a primitive golden age set in the past as well as being a golden world above that awaits us after death. Such is the interesting and curious vagueness of religious thought that the strangely blurred location of the golden world – its being linked with the past and tradition, with the present and the Above, *and* with the future beyond death, all at once – does not matter in the least. It passes quite unnoticed. It certainly does not make the golden world appear remote. We moderns habitually operate with very distinct and very long scales of time and space. To us, the beginnings of *homo sapiens* and 'a country far, far beyond the stars' sound very remote both from us and from each other, but for religious thought they were somehow one, and close. The heavenly world of tradition could actually be seen, for it was visible in stained glass, on the iconostasis and indeed simply in the liturgy in church. You visited the heavenly world every Sunday, joined its worship and conversed with its inhabitants. These glorious denizens of heaven were figures from the past and tradition who were now up above and whose company was your personal future. No problem. The heavenly world was somewhat like the aboriginal Dreamtime.[12] It was a mythical, magical immemorial world that pervaded this present world, and you could slip in and out of it at any time. Thirty years ago, I could do it. I lived in this earthly world of ours somehow with the guidance and help of the heavenly world to which I resorted constantly. It needs to be stressed that so potent is the Dreamtime that for me the sacred world truly was more vivid and real than the world of sense. And this living-through-a-dream was a thoroughly effective and perfectly functional way to live. I mean, it worked, it really did work.

God's authority over this life of ours was the authority of the Above over the below, of limitless power over weakness, of tradition and the older generation over the young, and of men over women. By contrast with God's vast age, wisdom and stability, young people are always seen as impetuous and undisciplined. They are violent unstable tearaways who need firm parental control. Woman is of course also perceived as inordinate and threatening, but she is treated as being even younger than youth. She is a child. Her weakness is constitutional: it is something like a natural fault for which she is not altogether to blame, so that it should be handled with indulgent but firmly protective kindness. Her misfortune is to be wayward, fickle and easily led. But there is something worse that makes her almost a potential demoness. Her passions are too strong for her, and in many or most cultures it is (or was) seriously believed that if she is fully sexually awakened she becomes insatiably and uncontrollably lustful to an extent that seriously threatens the social order.[13] So she has to be protected from herself and kept in perpetual childhood innocence, sheltered from reality. Until the nineteenth century women were minors almost everywhere. They still are, to a considerable extent.

Not surprisingly the full weight of cultural and religious pressure was brought to bear on those whose double misfortune it was to be both female and young. To this day even in Western countries it is still felt to be appropriate for a woman to be physically smaller and younger than her husband, so that she shall be treated with just a little (but a little is enough in these matters) of teasing and humouring, as if she were a child, a pet or a plaything. It is not at all incompatible with this régime that society should at the same time regard a reduced and damaged psychological state – anxious, hesitant, over-fastidious and abnormally lacking in self-confidence – as being the *normal* female psychology. And I need not add that just as society equates in a woman a particular kind of damage with 'goodness', so because we are all of us feminine in relation to God religion equates its own particular kind of psychological damage with piety. Just as in the social sphere the spectre of reckless female lust is used to warn us all to keep women in subjection, so in the religious sphere the doctrine of original sin is used to keep us in subjection by advising us of the fearful dangers of pride and

presumption. Every believer before God ought to behave something like a child-woman, and the church has a whole array of
father-figures to make the point.

In retrospect the belief that women are more dangerous than
men because their fickle passions threaten the very fabric of
society is very surprising. It can surely only have been so widely
held because the subjection of women was felt to be constitutive
of morality itself and of the entire social order, so that the direst
warnings were needed to keep it in place and unquestioned.
Religious conservatives today are probably correct in their
instinctive conviction that the subjection of women is central to
and has been constitutive of the religious and cultural systems
that we have inherited from the past. That is why the most
orthodox Jews, Christians and Muslims can come to terms with
virtually every aspect of ethical and political modernity – except
feminism. It and it alone is of the essence. Sexism is constitutive of
their whole world-view, and they cannot possibly abandon it.

This way of thinking was compounded by the venerable
defence mechanism that always leads us to blame not our own
impulses but whatever tempts us by provoking them. Woman is
to blame for being a provocation to man. Thus Judah the Pious, a
mystical writer of the Middle Ages, warns us of the way woman
tempts the righteous by hanging out her clothing on the
washing-line to dry.[14] It is her plain duty not to provoke us in this
manner. She should be thoroughly secluded, modest, chaste and
covered up, because every bit of her is a snare. Why, even her little
finger burns with lust. That there is projection going on here is
indicated by the fact that neither Judah the Pious nor any other of
a thousand male writers like him could ever dream of reversing
the argument and saying to themselves, 'If a woman is indeed
such an inordinately lustful creature and quite unable to control
herself, then *my* voice, *my* clothing, *my* little finger must be
unbearably provocative to her, so surely *I* am the one who should
become silent and secluded?' But nobody ever heard of a man
modestly veiling himself in order not to provoke women and lead
them into sin. So there must be projection at work here. The
psychological mechanism involved can lead to some pretty
surprising opinions. When in 1987 we became abruptly aware of
the extremity and seeming frequency of the gross and extraordinary sexual abuse of children I wondered how far the topic had a

traceable history in Judaeo-Christian culture. I found one allusion in ancient Jewish literature: fathers were enjoined to safeguard their sons because boys need to be protected from their own desire for strange men.[15] Men, it seems, are never to blame. It is the women and children who provoke them who are at fault.

To a much greater extent than we yet realize culture has been made possible by the concentration of power, which in turn has been made possible by the creation and idealization of radically unequal relationships – starting with the man-woman relationship. Man and woman, lord and handmaid, are a complete miniature society, indeed a complete miniature universe. And so far woman has borne the main burden of culture. Do we understand that woman paid for God? That is, the objectification of God, his enthronement in all his glory and majesty as the supreme power and principle of all things, is the exact counterpart of the subjection of woman. For there to be the one, there had to be the other. For him to be so powerful, she must be weak. For him to be so holy, she must be ritually unclean. For his creativity to be so absolute, her sexual energy and creativity had to be denied. For him to be so free and lordly, she must be content to be confined and ancillary (lit., 'hand-maidenly'). Woman's self-disparagement is the exact correlate of God's self-affirmation. Hence the wry comments that one often hears from women about the Lords of creation: they have an idea of the way in which they themselves were put down in order to make that lordship possible. For the whole system works precisely by putting woman in general and her sexuality in particular at the opposite pole from God. We all need God so much precisely because he does not need us at all; and the principle applies *especially* to women. Any suggestion that God could need a *female* around him, that he wants a consort, is blasphemous. Symbolically, woman is sex, and God is spiritualized away beyond sexuality. In Islam he is so far spiritualized as to be beyond even fatherhood. Though still masculine in gender, he is now just pure independent creative power. Femaleness is very far away from him. If a *woman* is to please a God who has so completely transcended sex, she must do it by denying her own sexuality and bodiliness with all her might and becoming something like an anorexic nun or a virgin mother. She must be utterly non-threatening, with as little self-esteem as possible. His being so high requires her to be that low. His being so absolutely One requires her to be inwardly divided, flesh against spirit.

Thus woman has paid the price. We human beings had to build societies and had to gain some sort of control over ourselves and our environment in order to survive. We had to find out what power was and how to concentrate it, so as first to build coherent societies and then to accumulate the technologies and knowledge-systems that would secure our survival. Woman was the first bit of nature man conquered. Man's knowledge, control and possession of women became the prime metaphor and model first for God's and then for man's knowledge, control and possession of the world, while at the same time woman's relation to man became a paradigm for the general human relation to God.

It follows from all this that historic Christianity, before the rise of humanitarianism, was not chiefly interested in human emancipation or in the Christianization of human social relationships. So far as its cultural mission was concerned it was interested almost exclusively in the construction and maintenance of hierarchies of power and control, angelic, imperial and ecclesiastical. Out of unequal relationships, joined up in vertical chains, a church, an Empire and a universe could be built. That is why *the religiously-significant human relationships*, from which we draw the special vocabulary of prayer, *are without exception highly unequal*. They are, principally, the relations of Lord to servant, King to subject, Judge to defendant and Father to son. Less common, but also found, are terms such as Master and Husband. The attributes of God are also set up in polar terms which stress and permutate the power-gap between God and the believer. In the Western vocabulary with which most of us are familiar the most frequently invoked contrasts are almighty-weak, holy-sinful, immortal-mortal, eternal-temporal, heavenly-earthly, unchanging-changing and unfailing-frequently failing. The aim of the language in every detail is first to spiritualize power by veiling the primitive sexual violence from which it starts, and then to concentrate and objectify it in God. Civilization is thus made possible, as authority and legitimacy flow down from God through Christ to the twin, complementary hierarchies of church and state. We scarcely need to remind ourselves of the extent to which the architecture, the dress, the iconography, the organization and the liturgy of the Latin church were derived directly from the later Roman Empire in general and from the Emperor-cult in particular. Though at the personal level classical Christianity was perceived as being about the purification of the self in preparation for the next life, in political terms it was about inequality and power. Where you have any unequal human relationship you have already a *micro-concentration* of power, the power for example of a father over his child or of a man over his wife. Religion picks up such relationships, joins them up in ascending chains, spiritualizes them, and so creates even greater and more awesome concentrations of power.

This discussion has now given us a way of formulating the contrast between classical Christianity and the modern religion that has been developing since the Enlightenment. Classical Christianity was about power. It regarded inequality of power in human relationships as a positively good thing, a religiously-significant thing, and indeed as providing it with the raw material out of which it could build its world. By contrast, modern Christianity is humanitarian. It is interested in rights, that is, in finding ways of helping, strengthening and revaluing all those who are in various ways at a disadvantage. It doesn't reject power, but it does want to see power more evenly distributed and circulating more freely. It wants to disperse established concentrations of power such as God, the self, the political 'super-powers' and the church hierarchies. It wants a more fluid, decentred and mobile world, in which power and creativity are not fixed in certain hierarchies but instead flow freely, available to all. Where classical Christianity found inequality and ordered gradations of power exciting, we need to be developing a religion that finds equality and spontaneity exciting.

To some extent this is already happening. Modern Christianity has started to get interested in human rights, in social ethics, in the Christianization of secular human relationships, in striving to better the conditions of life of the poorest, and so on. Fine – but completely at variance with the theology and the structures inherited from the past. It is utterly unthinkable that there should be any appeal against the decrees of Calvin's God, or any place for the idea of human rights in his system. Roman Catholic canon law and church structures make Stalinism seem positively liberal. It is preposterous that our daily practices in prayer and worship should so flagrantly contradict the concern for human dignity and freedom that church leaders sincerely profess when they get on their hind legs in public. The fact is that if modern humanitarian Christianity is ever to become established and to assert itself consistently then it must sooner or later purge itself of cosmic feudalism.

Although it has become very ramshackle, the old feudalism still dominates theology, worship, prayer and patterns of organization. People excuse it all by saying that because it is all now so ramshackle it doesn't actually do much harm any more; but that is a mistake, like the mistake of supposing that because the British monarchy has not got much political clout any longer it cannot be doing any harm. But on the contrary, in the postmodern world, which is so largely made of signs, what really counts is how large you bulk on the mediascape – and *there* the royal family are bigger than ever, not just in Britain but around much of the world. By the same token a good many now-obsolete and noxious religious ideas, rituals and institutions continue to have considerable imaginative and symbolic power, the power that really counts now. They should be purged. If we are sincerely committed to the new more humane and this-worldly kind of Christianity then of course we must try to expel these relics of a very ugly past.

Easier said than done, no doubt. What is called for is a religion fully committed to the here and now. A religion that, amazingly, finds equality and not inequality sexy. A religion that loves free-flowing spontaneous creativity. A religion that doesn't inhabit a fantasy-world but whose domain coincides with the only world there is, namely the here-and-now world of signs, the world of communication. This then means dispersing God into people, people into their own communicative activities, and the cosmos into an unceasing, endlessly self-renewing process of communal artistic production. *Our* work of art.

Religion in that world will be a way of celebrating a human emancipation that is continually to be striven for and realized afresh. For the christianized version of a postmodern world that I am describing cannot be suddenly realized once and for all and then fixed as a permanent achievement. Rather, it has itself to be a continuous productive activity, which is why there needs to be a continual re-enactment of the liturgy (*leitourgia*, public service) of religion.

We will picture a postmodern eucharist as a ceremonial enactment of the death and dispersal of God. God goes out into language, that is, into humanity. He passes out into multiplicity and, dying, communicates his power and creativity to us. Thus the Law comes to an end and Gospel takes its place, for by 'the Law' I just mean the hierarchized disciplinary universe that people inhabited during the entire historical period, and which has so recently come to an end. Yes, we certainly recycle the past, but we do so ironically; yes, we love nostalgia and revivals, but our very ability to revive all earlier periods, we now see, shows that we are no longer locked into a period that is specifically our own in the way everyone used to be. Not locked into one period, being now too ironical and pluralistic for that, we cannot now be *held* so rigorously by the Law as people once were. We know there are many alternatives, so we know that those other possibilities are options open to us. So we come to the knowledge that *we* made all those other options, and now it is only a matter of time before we grasp that we made the Law itself and it too is optional. And now we are free from the Law, because it has ceased to be absolute. Everything is permitted – including an optional, ironical return to the Law – and nothing is objectively obligatory.

We are free because we are not constrained by period, by history, and by the Law in the way we were. In the ancient cyclical and dispensational systems world-history passed through a series of theologically-qualified epochs. What you could do and become was largely predetermined by the theological character of the age into which you had been born. The 'period' thinking that perhaps began with the Centuriators of Magdeburg (*Historia Ecclesiae Christi*, Basel 1559–1574) was not very different. History was the age of grace that God had allowed to us human beings between Pentecost and the end of the world.[16] It was divisible into a series of centuries, presumably twenty or so in all, though in their volumes Flacius and his colleagues covered only the first thirteen. But God had decided that all those centuries were going to be dominated by just one theme only; the Gospel was going to get steadily weaker as the Papal Antichrist grew steadily stronger. The main script was already written. If you lived in one of those centuries, the totality to which your life-work would be a contribution had already been determined. Thus you were rather strictly constrained by period, in that God had set in advance the limits of what your life could amount to.

But our postmodern age is Christian and eschatological in that *we* find ourselves living in a strange open-textured period after the end of period, after history and the Law, and therefore after the death of the old Almighty One who formerly concentrated and absorbed all power into himself. The huge diffusion of information this century has made us all so pluralistic, so knowing, so ironical that everything has been dispersed, even God. God has brought history to an end by dying, by giving himself to us, returning his power of defining reality into *us*. We are no longer within a period whose theological character has been antecedently defined for us by him. Or rather, the special theological character of the present age is its *absence* of any impressed theological character. This freedom, this openness and *lack of any destiny* which has resulted from God's own voluntary self-dispersal marks our own queer post-'period'-period as the first truly *Christian* period. We are emancipated because we are not stuck with any ready-made destiny. We are not on rails of any kind.[17] All the *grands récits*, the great narratives, have passed away. Our future is open. It is for us to make. This is the real Age of Grace, after history. And it is what our eucharist must celebrate.

5

STRATEGIES FOR CHRISTIAN SURVIVAL

(a) Inside the church

It seems that we must belong to the church and that nevertheless we cannot belong to the church. We must belong because in our view the self is primarily social and linguistic, and religion is primarily social and linguistic. A tradition, a vocabulary and a community – these three things belong together, and they come first. There is no bypassing them. If we think that religion deals with important questions not properly addressed elsewhere, then, whatever we may eventually find we want to say in it, we will need to learn the religious vocabulary written into our own tradition. So we need to belong to the church. We have no other place to start from. Whether we are docile or dissident members of the family, it is only within that family's disputatious common life that we can express ourselves properly. One-man religion is madness: however radical our theology gets to be, it can only be sane and sensible and of interest to others if it presents itself as a continuation and an interpretation of traditional faith. A religion is a language, and the faith of today and tomorrow has got to be the legitimate child of yesterday's faith just as a good modern prose style has got to be an appropriate modification of traditional styles. We cannot start entirely from scratch. We've got to work within a tradition; so we've got to belong to the church and learn its language before we can find ways of bending that language to meet modern needs.

Yet surely we *cannot* belong to the church? For one thing, it regards our views as beyond the pale. With its God and its heavenly world, the church evokes a settled peaceful universe, hierarchized, centred and controlled, a home to live in. But we say that precisely all that is dead. We have lost all supernatural realities, we have lost the eternal world above, we have lost objective purposefulness, meanings and moral realities in the world, and – most important – we have lost the objective correspondences between different aspects of reality that sustained traditional Christian symbolism. As a result an extraordinarily complete and comprehensive death of religious and metaphysical language has been taking place during the present century. Our life, our world and our history have altogether lost their old external support. But unfortunately traditional faith was mainly expressed in terms of how our life is seen, judged and sustained from outside. So it has gone up in smoke.

We are now getting over the initial reaction of despair, pessimism and nihilism, and many people think we can already see what will emerge from the wreckage of the old West: the world will come to be seen as a vast flowing process of what the scientists call events and the arts people signs. Call it something like a Buddhist or a relativist vision of things, with a non-cognitive religious discipline and an ethic of 'environmental agapism'. A green process-Christianity, perhaps. Content to be immersed in natural cycles and artistic production, people will have forgotten the old idea of a march of history that was supposed to be getting somewhere. They will be living at the end of time, after history.

Along some such lines as these the faith of the future is perhaps beginning to take shape, but it is going to be very difficult during the next century to bend existing economic, political and religious systems so as to adapt them to the new conditions. Individuals, though, are already making adjustments. When there is no great goal of life, no timeless world of unseen realities and no hereafter, I am forced into the present. Having no long-term future, I must find eternity in the ephemeral. The message is inevitably rather Buddhist: to be thus inwardly voided, to lose one's own inner substantiality, anchorage and destiny, is to be pushed towards a very cool *ecstasis*. When I have no self then I stand outside myself. And arguably all this is Christian. At least, it can easily be illustrated from the tradition of Christian mysticism.

At present, however, the church utterly repudiates all these ideas, and any suggestion that it needs to modernize itself. In fact it is headed in the opposite direction. Just as in the nineteenth century

Judaism emerged rather abruptly from the Middle Ages, was plunged into the modern world, and in fear of losing its own identity turned to various kinds of Zionism and ultra-Orthodoxy, so the church too has been trying to resist its own creeping disappearance by assimilation. It ghettoizes itself, turns itself into a subculture and reaffirms evangelical theology or neo-Thomism or biblical theology. It gets more sacerdotal and sacramental. It is willing to try absolutely anything that will help it to preserve what it takes to be its own essential doctrines in their purest form. The minimum requirement, in order to keep traditional orthodoxy on the road, is that there shall be a realistic metaphysics of two worlds, a lower visible one and a higher, timeless and invisible one; and that there shall be spiritual substances, finite and infinite. This in turn means that the church must stipulate that the philosophical outlook of Plato and Artistotle has got to be kept going for ever. Probably the maximum concession to modernity that can be made is that orthodox Christianity is perhaps expressible without too drastic a change in terms of the early, modern classicism of Descartes.

That particular issue is finely balanced. Descartes himself considered that his own philosophy was the right vehicle for catholic Christianity in a scientific age, and many very able people have agreed with him. Rome, however, was always dubious, and various neo-Thomists such as Etienne Gilson have made out a strong case against Descartes.[1] If they are right then it really is Plato and Aristotle forever, in which case the church must turn itself into a closed cult. It must become the Jehovah's Witnesses. It doesn't want us. We represent everything that it is in flight from.

So we need the church – as a community, a vocabulary, a starting-point, something that we are proposing eventually to transform. But the church does not in the least wish to be changed and will have none of this. Things are not going to go our way in the church for a long time yet, if ever. So how can we stay in the church if we feel, or she feels, that we are at odds with her traditional faith? We need some sort of strategy for medium-term survival. Three such strategies deserve to be considered: evasion, deception and open, organized dissent. The *evader* uses various devices to play down difficulties of faith and stop them from becoming too prominent. The stratagems used may be largely unconscious. The *deceiver*, often a theologian, avoids detection and censure by using a fully-traditional vocabulary, but craftily exploits its flexibility in order to make it say extremely untraditional things. The *dissenters* think it most honest to organize themselves as a campaigning movement or party. They try to establish a common front and fight for general acceptance of their point of view as a legitimate option within the church.

Evasion

Scientific ideas are easy to criticize because they don't bite back. Religious ideas are altogether different. God is an all-knowing person who sees everything and forgets nothing. He searches your thoughts, detecting the slightest impulse of criticism or revolt long before you do yourself, and the punishments he inflicts are terrible beyond your worst imaginings. Thus in many ways the ideas of God, sin, judgment and hell seem to have been specially designed to protect the authority of orthodoxy by frightening people away from questioning it.[2] Certainly many people find the thought that they themselves may be approaching unbelief or heresy utterly terrifying. It fills them with the fear of damnation, the worst psychological state there is. To protect itself, the psyche will tend to steer us away from dangerous ground. That is what I mean by a strategy of evasion. It is a largely-unconscious strategy of avoiding conflict by remaining inexplicit and not thinking dangerous thoughts. A strong instinct for surviving and avoiding trouble leads us to repress doubt, to refrain from cultivating it or to take up theologies that craftily conceal it.

A few examples: most preaching today is symbolist, hortatory and doctrinally very vague. A large proportion of the sermons I hear – and I hear many – are entirely compatible with my own completely demythologized and anti-realist viewpoint. Indeed, the realization that they are in agreement with me without realizing it is very encouraging to me. But the preachers themselves think they are orthodox, and indeed nobody would dream of impugning their orthodoxy. What can be going on in such a case? It seems that these preachers are remaining within the fold in good conscience by not permitting themselves to become too explicit about the philosophical status of their own language. They don't follow through. They stay orthodox by averting their eyes and not becoming aware of what they don't want to know. In this they resemble the many Jungian Christians who take up Jung's ideas with a great sense of relief and without remarking that the religious liberation that Jung can undoubtedly give is in fact liberation *from* orthodoxy and realistic faith. Technically, Jung is relativistic in that for him all religions are true, and he is naturalistic in that for him the truth of religion is a purely human truth, an imaginative, symbolic or psychological truth. Religious ideas are not objectively true but only subjectively true, which is to say that they are psychologically helpful, which is to say that they are comforting. But Jungian Christianity wouldn't work if it were too explicit, and it would be wrong to describe Jungianism as 'atheistic'. It would be more accurate (if *accurate* is the word) to say that Christian Jungianism is a religion or a theology for people who are pursuing a strategy of evasion. Jung himself carefully laid a few false trails, as if towards the end of his life he had recognized that people cannot bear too much consciousness. So he kindly designed an interesting form of religious naturalism, with a little unconsciousness included within it, that could be taken up in good conscience by Christians with problems.

Another example of evasion is what used to be called 'the retreat into history' as practised by many theologians of the past hundred years. One avoids theology proper, and confines oneself to writing about the past. It is an easy move and very popular, especially in association with the positivist belief that it is possible and desirable to recover the original meaning of the text, purely objectively and without any superadded element of interpretation. One can, as it were, have the past *pure*. And most theologians are in fact critical historians who study and interpret texts from the past. They are students of the Bible, of the history of doctrine, of church history and so forth, and they need never attempt constructive utterance *in propria persona*. Indeed, those whom media people believe to be conservative theologians are almost always historians who by celebrating the past have built up for themselves a great reputation for orthodoxy without ever actually producing any substantial arguments or affirmations on their own account. They have paid tribute to some past epoch or figure, and they have maybe sharply attacked the present leadership in the church for having been so spineless as to have permitted the modern world to come into existence. But at that point they have stopped, to be rewarded by tumultuous applause. They certainly don't propose to go on to tackle the question of what, given that the modern world has arrived and must be lived in, an honest person is now to believe and do and hope for. They do not tackle that question because they are evaders. They have found their own personal solution, by disappearing into the past. Imaginatively, they inhabit some age when the Christian intellectual could more easily profess the faith of the church in full than is possible now. By this simple expedient conservative church historians think that they have worked their own passage. They are themselves wholly orthodox – so long as they stay in the past.

Evasion became most highly developed as a strategy during the heyday of biblical theology in the period (approximately) 1930–1960. In 1979 the most eminent British churchman of the postwar years, by then very aged, preached for the last time in my College Chapel. He still preached the biblical theology of Cambridge in the 1930s. We heard him tell of a heavenly world above where the ascended Christ reigned in glory, seated at the right hand of God. Now this was craftier than at first appears. The distinguished preacher was expounding scripture. At a certain level what he was saying was all descriptively true and there was no basis for questioning his integrity, because after all it is descriptively the case that everything that he was saying could be found in the letters of Paul and the letter *To the Hebrews*, and it is also descriptively the case that this is the church's faith and what preachers are supposed to preach. By tacitly putting everything he said under the rubrics *scripture says . . .* and *the church teaches . . .* the preacher saved *both* his personal integrity (Yes, it's quite true, scripture does say this, and the church does indeed teach it) *and* his professional integrity as a minister of the Gospel, for the church after all commands us ministers to proclaim nothing but what she and scripture teach. What is missing? How could I get any leverage against this biblical theology?

Of course, I wanted to say that just reiterating the theology of St Paul is not preaching at all, but an evasion. I wanted to ask the usual tomfool questions like, Where is this 'ascended Christ'? I mean, is he a bloke out there? What's heaven, what's glory, what *is* the right hand of God? Until all this talk has been tied into our late-twentieth-century experience, way of life, language and world-picture we cannot do anything with it. It is like a disengaged cog that moves without doing any work. Words are being uttered, but nothing's getting said. But the obvious vulgarity and impertinence of my questions only showed how for English-establishment biblical theology inexplicitness was good manners and therefore orthodoxy. I was out of place.

An odd survival of biblical theology, which throws an interesting sidelight on what is wrong with it, can be seen in the following anecdote. A talented theologian, an eloquent and interesting figure, became all too explicit, declared for atheism and renounced his Orders. But he continued to teach biblical theology. To this day he can lecture on the theology of St Paul to an audience of Evangelicals without turning a hair. What he delivers purely historically they receive dogmatically, and they cordially approve him. The oddity of this is that somewhere the gearchange between historical assertion about what Paul wrote and personal confession of what we believe has become lost. Very curious – but biblical theology just *was* curious in that way.

The evasions I have been describing – woolly preaching, Jungianism, the retreat into history and biblical theology – usually require a certain innocent unconsciousness. We can recognize them in operation in other people, but the very act of spelling out what they are and how they work is liable to put them out of our own reach. One cannot deliberately adopt the little bit of unconsciousness required.

Also, the combination of a bit of unconsciousness with good conscience means that these little evasion-strategies are quietistic. They help people survive in the church, but don't actually do anything to change the church. The same is true of the commonest and simplest of all the evasions, just repressing your doubts and keeping your mouth shut. That too changes nothing.

Deception

Of more interest are those strategies for survival, and indeed for Christian renewal, which involve deliberate deception. The basic argument for deception is that we will only be able to overcome and outwit the orthodox if we practise a conscious deception more cunning than the many forms of unconscious self-deception practised by them and their fellow-travellers, the evaders. Recent literary theory has shown that absolute personal integrity, pure *oratio recta*, is a myth. Now, therefore, we need a theological version of Derrida's subtle battle against Absolute Reason, a battle in which there must be deception.

A simple example: as I suggested earlier, much preaching today, perhaps *most* of it, is compatible with radical views, even though the preachers themselves can't see it. If I had always preached like them I could both hold my own views and be applauded by the orthodox. Wouldn't that be nice? But I cannot work my own way back to acceptance by such a device, for I have come out and am marked for life. However, I can and sometimes do advise the young to be strategically inexplicit, 'deceivers and yet true'. It is so very easy: I advise them to do it while they are learning the game, until they are old and strong enough to come out having fully calculated what it means and what it will cost for them to come out. I face a risk here, because although some will doubtless come out in due course, as I think one should, many will decide along with Browning's Bishop Bloughram that inexplicitness and mild deception is really rather comfortable.

Bloughram makes the case for never coming out.[3] If he is right, one does not *have* to rock the boat. If you feel nevertheless that you have got to rock it, then he and those like him who have decided that it is not necessary to do so, and will do no good anyway, will be the first to condemn you for your folly and presumption. Why didn't you keep quiet like the rest of us? On your own head be it.

Here I simply disagree with Bishop Bloughram. I cannot recommend a lifetime strategy of deliberate and self-interested inexplicitness or deception, because it means losing one's soul. Any policy of planned deception, if adopted, must be adopted in order to change the church. The deceiver uses the traditional language of faith in order in the long run to argue people out of a traditional understanding of faith. He tries to change people's thinking without their realizing it. But it is not right to deceive merely in order to keep oneself comfortable.

Nor, at least in my view, is it right to pursue within the church a strategy whose real end is extra-ecclesiastical. For example, at least some of those involved in the campaign for the ordination of women to the priesthood and the episcopate are primarily interested not in any religious goal but in securing a symbolic victory for the feminist cause. When they have won they may well lose interest in the church, and if they lose they will certainly leave it.

I too am a deceiver in this matter, with an ulterior motive, but in a somewhat different way. I am a deceiver because, as has been said already, I oppose the traditional sharp demarcation between the clergy and the laity, and the many-tiered hierarchy within the church. It creates a severe imbalance in the distribution of power within the church, freezes power within a structure, and has skewed the whole of theology towards the task of legitimating clerical power. Too great a preoccupation with institutionalized spiritual power makes for thoroughly bad religion. In the most extreme case, the Christian life becomes dominated by a Pope-cult that makes one squirm. The fact is that the ecclesiastical polity of the principal churches is nothing but spiritual Tsarism. In the USSR at the time of writing, people are saying that after a millennium of authoritarian government, serfdom and personality-cults the only way the country can grow up is by the development of robust democratic convictions in each and every citizen. Just so, and it's exactly the same with the church. So we advocate the admission of women to the hierarchy not in order to strengthen the hierarchy, but in the hope of weakening it. The hierarchy is masculinist; women members will confuse it intellectually and eventually undermine it. In the past the rule of men over women has been the paradigm case of an intelligible, divinely-ordained, cosmically-significant inequality. It provided a building-brick which, metaphorically extended, permutated and multiplied, was used to erect social structures and knowledge-systems. So our cosmology, our theology and indeed the whole of culture became highly patriarchal, and the upshot is that today the church is the chief surviving monument and bastion of patriarchy and its world-view. The advancement of women to the priesthood and the episcopate within the church deserves support because it is a cause which has a chance of succeeding, and which if it does succeed will undermine the ideological stronghold of patriarchy and so do more than anything else could to prepare the way for the modernization of Christianity.

For many feminists, just getting women into a traditional male bastion is an end in itself, a symbolic victory that has to be won. For me it's a means towards the greater end of achieving a modern post-patriarchal Christianity, beyond God the Father.

This brings us to the question of deception about God. For the sake of continuity, and in order to help people to cross the bridge, we *have* to be deceivers in theology – as theologians know well. Religious idioms are very flexible, and all parties exploit their flexibility. People say you can prove anything from the Bible; similarly, you can do almost anything in theology, and a good thing too. Here is a first and simple example: When a journalist or interviewer asks, 'Do you believe in life after death?', I have for some years replied, 'Yes: I am living it *now* because, as St Paul teaches, we died and rose with Christ in our baptism. The Christian life is *already* life after death.' Is my reply a straight deception? It is true that I fail to affirm life after death in the sense the questioner had in mind, so that many will say I should have answered with an honest No. However, that would in effect have left the questioner feeling that for me our life is even more worthless than it is for those who believe in life after death, for it has been robbed of the compensatory aftermath that used to brighten it up a bit. So the negative answer produces a very downbeat effect, which is not what I really intend. By answering in the affirmative I try to get the questioner to see our *present* life as having something of the eternal glory and beauty that he thought could be found only after death. So I try to produce an upbeat effect. Am I then a deceiver? Of course I don't believe that we shall live again after we have died. But I *do* believe in life after death in the sense that for a truly religious person who has 'died with Christ' and thereby has become able to love life, people and things without egoistic anxiety – for such a person, this life of ours can have all the value that people once located in Heaven or the Kingdom of God. By my reply I am in effect saying, 'I won't answer your question straight, because I think you are asking the wrong question. Try looking at it this way instead: You think that to make it worthwhile our life needs a reward or a compensation after death, but I'm saying that we ourselves can and should change in such a way that that need no longer arises. So I suggest that the life after death you feel you need can be and is *now*, and I back up my claim by referring to Paul's teaching about baptism. Die and rise with Christ, now. This life should be lived as if after death.'

Just how deceitful is this? I don't give straight answers to straight questions, because theology isn't a matter of getting people to believe a few extra things. Religious language is therapeutic. We aim to use it to bring about a shift of perspective, so that people shall no longer have wrong questions preying on their minds.

What of the case of God? It is very similar. Just as people falsely reify eternal life as an extra life after our life, so they falsely reify God. God becomes a big, big friendly guy out there whom you can confide in, or he becomes a demonic persecuting Father in the Unconscious, or he becomes a bit of both. At any rate, prayer is understood dualistically as talking to somebody else and 'Do you believe in God?' is made to mean, 'Do you think that there is a great invisible Spirit out there independent of us, who would still be there even if all of us and the whole world were to cease to exist?'[4] But to the question as thus phrased many great figures and texts are reluctant to give a straight and unqualified answer. They prefer to try to change the way we think. In particular they want to modify the idioms in which we speak of God. The New Testament, or part of it at least, seems to say: 'Don't think of God as an infinitely-great One Out There, but think of God instead as one who is in Christ, and as one who is poured out into our hearts as Spirit. God is *in us*, God dwells in our hearts.' Metaphor; but it seems to mean that God is now not a being, but a human thought, value, ideal or capacity. The Quakers say that there is something of God in every one. Metaphor; but an influential interpretation of what it means is 'Treat each person as if he or she were the God, the bearer of sovereign and inalienable rights that have to be respected.' F. H. Bradley says that God has no meaning outside of the religious consciousness.[5] Wittgenstein says that the question of God is not a question about the existence of something, but rather a question about the place of religious ideas in our lives and about the work that the word 'God' does in our speech.[6] Jung says God is an archetype in the Unconscious, the greater Self that we are to become, the goal of our life.[7] St John says God is just love. Dietrich Bonhoeffer says that in Christianity God has become weak, God has been edged out, and in theology we should follow Christ and move from Heaven to earth and from God to man.[8] Kierkegaard, in a famous definition of faith, said that our very doubt and our objective uncertainty about God, if clung to with sufficient passion, will do the trick for us religiously just as well as the old confidence about God.[9] Taking similar ideas a stage further, I have said that a sense of the absence of God is the same thing as a sense of the presence of God. I have also said, 'Don't think of God as an objective being, think of God instead as having many names – death, otherness, the void, difference, Christ, the Good, love – in short, whatever makes us realize our own utter transience and imperfection.' The idea is still Kierkegaardian. It is, *that there is no God is also God*, or, just the thought of the Void or of the impossibility of perfection can do the job of God for us, which is to unself us.

In all these writers the theme is the same. God gets objectified by the demand of the clerics for real sanctions and for real legitimation of their authority. That is why they are theological realists. God also gets objectified by our own religious fear and guilt. But the whole point of the Gospel is that it is supposed to be a liberation from the fear of that authoritarian, guilt-inducing Power-God. Gospel preaching is the struggle against theological realism. So when people ask, 'Is there a God?', the Christian teacher shouldn't answer yes or no but should turn back upon the questioner and try to remove the wrong idea of God that gave rise to the question. And indeed I have on occasion been willing to take the deliberately-flummoxing and deceitful use of religious language so far as to declare that 'Atheism is God'. The point is simple: *Christian* god-talk has to be a way of release from religious terror. That which saves us from the fear of damnation is what properly deserves to be called God. Some people are thus saved by atheism. For them therefore atheism is God.

Some critics say that we theologians speak with forked tongues, using forms of words that mean one thing to conservatives and something else to liberals. We equivocate, by trying to say something interesting while simultaneously protecting our flanks. The critics urge that we should always give straight answers and admit what we literally believe. But I am saying that there is no such thing as literal truth and no such thing as 'the real meaning' of any text. Church authority has in the past sought for power reasons to control religious language, but such control is 'the letter that killeth' and is death to religion. Religious terms do not stand for, label or copy religious objects. Religion consists in a change in the way we see everything, a change in our whole life. The religious teacher *must* use language manipulatively, rhetorically and deceitfully in order to bring about that change. And if as we have argued it is true that today large-scale and general religious change is needed, then we'll have to be deceivers to bring it about. If the church is to have a future at all we must belong to her, and we must take diabolical liberties with her language, bending it into hitherto-unheard-of shapes. We must be Zen.

Organized dissent

The third option for radicals is to organize. We believe that our survival in the church is a matter of consequence, because upon it hinges the church's own survival. We should associate, work out a common platform and campaign; and our aim in doing so is not merely to achieve a concessionary recognition of our own right to exist within the church. We want to win, because if we don't the various sorts of traditionalist will succeed in their objective of converting the church into a steadily-declining closed cult.

There's the rub. We claim to be the people who are *opposed* to factionalism. We are against the historic Christian preoccupation with concentrating spiritual power and wielding it over other people. We oppose the conversion of religious beliefs into items of political ideology, and we do not wish to inhabit a confraternity of the embattled like-minded. To form a *party*, with a party line and agreed objectives, is surely contrary to everything we profess? We wish to be varied and scattered individuals each doing our own thing in our own way, like artists and writers. Perhaps, if the time is ripe, what we are all doing will add up to a ferment. But these things cannot and must not be forced. Since we do not actually approve either of concentrated and hierarchized religious power or of parties formed to struggle for it, we should not occupy ourselves with building a party machine to advance our cause. We shouldn't even think of ourselves as *having* a cause, because such a thought is corrupting. And in any case, the history of earlier Modernist movements in the church is not encouraging. They failed to change the church, and they broke down internally because of their own contradictions. Others, such as twice-born Fundamentalists, morality campaigners, Catholics and Calvinists may self-consistently seek power and control, and may use a disciplined campaigning party or pressure-group as their vehicle. But Modernists, radicals and ultra-liberals cannot work in such a way. We are anarchists. We love freedom and mobility. We don't want creeds, discipline, parties and power-struggles. By nature we are civilians, not soldiers.

Under present conditions the happiest way to avoid these

difficulties is to be a lay person who is an occasional religious conformist. The church's disciplinary control over the laity is rather weak nowadays. It has been allowed to slacken because the laity have no power and therefore do not matter. They can be left alone. This in turn makes it easy for a layperson to keep in touch with the church, to utilize it as a spiritual resource, and to be occasionally observant without the risks of moral corruption that come with being got at, drawn in, committed or becoming involved with the power-structure. Present conditions make such semi-detached church membership easy, and it is precisely what millions of laypeople understandably opt for. They can maintain contact with traditional religion while otherwise being left enviably free to do their own postmodern thing in lifestyle, in work, in ethical or artistic production or whatever. The left hand keeps a traditional rhythm going somewhere in the background, while the right hand plays a free personal variation upon it.

Lucky people. Unfortunately, such a solution may not be available for very much longer. In the advanced countries at least, the church contracts by one per cent per annum or so. Penumbral layperson's Christianity may be fine for the individual, for now, but it will not save the church. For the sake of the clergy and of those laypeople who care about the future of the church, and indeed for the sake of the church herself, there will probably have to be an organization. To avoid contradictions, it cannot be a party and it cannot have a creed. But it can be a fellowship and a forum, concerned not with fighting its own corner but with evolving the future form of the church.

This future form of the church will be a new order of personal relationships. How can the church both become for the first time really free and plural, and continue to be coherent and robust enough as a society to make a significant impact in politics and public life? So far, what people speak of as 'strength' in society has been built up by aggregating and amplifying the power-over-another that is wielded in unequal human relationships. These unequal human relationships, so far as they settle into a pattern, are always recognizably marital: master and man, officer and batman, craftsman and mate, boss and secretary, Holmes and Watson, Wooster and Jeeves, abbot and prior, General and ADC. The power wielded in such relationships is the same as that which is wielded in the family, namely, sexual aggression and will-to-dominate, variously evoked, hallowed, restrained, institutionalized, sublimated and channelled by culture. Society recognizes that in these relationships, the assistant, the Sancho Panza, the Figaro, the 'wife', is very often the smarter of the two, more in touch with reality and emotionally more resilient; but the 'cosmic' inequality remains the prime fact. Our traditional religious and cultural systems, including classical Christianity, were chiefly about that prime fact. That is to say, the basic fact of life, namely sexual domination, was hyped up, mythicized, multiplied, made cosmic. Controlled, yes, to some extent, but also validated – by God the Father.

The outcome today is that it feels as if the whole of culture in the past was, and the psychology that it has bequeathed to us still is, profoundly sado-masochistic. We have just discovered what savages we have always been hitherto. Our past has made us creatures for whom only inequality is sexy. That is, we feel that everywhere in our social relations and in the cosmos the one and only thing that can bind two parties together really effectively is radical inequality of power between them. It is their inequality of power that makes the patient fall in love with the analyst, the hostage with the hijacker, and the prisoner with the interrogator. Equality cannot really *bind*. There is no deep love-bonding without enslavement. The relationship has to be tilted towards one party, who seizes power and uses it to subjugate the other – and thus we have a miniature society, the beginnings of a world.

It is a striking fact that well into the present century Freud and Sartre were still adhering to the classic assumption of theism-monarchy-patriarchy: someone must rule, someone must wear the trousers, someone must be the boss. Sartre at least in his early work, and Freud always, still saw the world in terms of dominance and subjection and to that extent they were both of them still theists. Dominance is creative, it is what makes the world – such is the message. For a brief period Lou Salome tempted Freud to abandon his principles, but otherwise all his life he was like God: he couldn't abide an equal.

Yet Freud must have known that the West already had a tradition that found equality religiously significant. Among Romantics such as Hölderlin, Hegel and Wordsworth we meet the theme of yearning after an ideal soulmate and sister, companion and better half, an alter ego who is different but equal, other than me and yet the same as me, my counterpart, my twin. The brother-sister relationship, now more highly idealized that it had ever previously been, comes to be presented as the perfect human relationship, closer even than marriage.

Why were the Romantics willing to risk the charge that they were somehow promoting incest? One must recall that a number of them were people of the highest talent. Someone like Kierkegaard had to spend his whole life without ever encountering an equal, and was acutely conscious of the loneliness to which his gifts condemned him. To such a person meeting a twin soul could be an extraordinarily thrilling and joyous experience, something to dream about. It was difficult to picture heterosexual marriage as a relation of equals. A number of feminists themselves argued that a heterosexual relationship could *never* be equal. They thought, as Andrea Dworkin does today, that heterosexual intercourse is an act of subjugation. (This is what Genesis 3.16b seems to say, and what many men and children seem to believe.) So, in search of an image of the sought-after unity of the self with its own Other or Double, the Romantics went back to the innocent brother-sister relationship of childhood. And many a nineteenth-century man reports a peculiar exaltation of the spirit that he felt when he met a woman whom he knew at once was in every way fully his equal. And the theme, found also in Feuerbach, that 'when equals meet, God is incarnate' is extended in Romantic thought to the relation of a person to her own soul, and the relation of man to nature. God becomes included also because in Romantic thought the fully-realized horizontal reconciliation of each with all and of all with each simply coincides with the final self-manifestation of God.

During the nineteenth century the Romantic dream that there might be a spiritually exalting friendship, complementarity and equality between the sexes underwent some elaboration in social theory and even found some embodiment in social practice. But it is worth recalling that 'sexism' is a coinage of the late 1960s, and that even at that date was still greeted with a good deal of honest bewilderment. Many men couldn't for the life of them see what 'sexism' was supposed to *be*. Before we could fully grasp the concept and its ramifications, a whole lot of lines of thought had to come together: Freud, semiotics, 'micro-power' and a good deal of feminist culture-criticism.

These things *have* now come together. We can now begin to see – for example, in the very strong public resistance during the present century to the step-by-step discovery that the family is very far from being an innocent social unit – just how well-defended and brutally sexist are the cultural systems that we have inherited. Having been produced by and adapted to serve a sexist culture, our inherited religious systems are also uncompromisingly, even ruthlessly, domineering. We are suggesting that a new order of personal relationships is needed, and that the Romantics and many of the early humanists and anarchists of the nineteenth century can still supply inspiration. If radical Christians organize themselves, it should not be to fight for a new creed, but rather in order to discover a new basis for human relationships.

(b) Outside the church

Self-imposed exile

'One of the things you and I have to learn,' said Wittgenstein to Con Drury, 'is that we have to live without the consolation of belonging to a church.'[10] To a philosopher, who must be a lover of doubt and freedom, all organizations are suspect, but the church has particular problems of her own. In the modern period culture has become fragmented and privatized. Conviction has gone out of the public realm, and it is no longer possible to acknowledge the great public objects or to act publicly 'for the glory of God' in quite the old way. As a result of this, the church's dogma and her worship have become oddly anachronistic and uncomfortable to us. There is something wrong about the grandiose and compulsory objectivity that dogma claims, which 'puts a brake on thinking'. Religious liberalism and crude apologetics are unendurably misguided, and the decline of the public realm has left too much of church language sounding hackneyed and repetitive. Wittgenstein could therefore bear only the most fleeting contacts with organized religion. He thought it best to follow Tolstoy's example and live in self-imposed exile from the church. A number of other writers, including Dostoyevsky and Kierkegaard in the nineteenth century, and Simone Weil and Iris Murdoch in more recent times, have taken a rather similar line.

Exile, however, is relative. The view of the self's relation to language and culture that we have been putting forward for some years makes it obvious that there can be no Christianity that is *wholly* outside the church. The religion of an exile, who is partly cut off, must be somewhat reduced and such substance as it retains will need to be nourished by communication with the main body. The lines of communication may run through memory, through the printed word or through friendships, but they have to be there. And if in this way lifelines back to the main tradition must after all be kept, what was the point of making the gesture of going into exile in the first place?

Some of the figures I have named would have said that for them it was a matter of honesty. They would mention three main stumbling-blocks: theological realism, dogmatic theology and ecclesiastical power. On the question of *theological realism* we hear from them something like this: 'The church undoubtedly takes a realistic view of God as a powerful personal Spirit upon whom the world depends for its existence, and who is out there whether we believe in him or not. Now I see the value of belief in God as a vehicle for our ideals, as supplying a transcendent perspective upon our lives and as at least notionally unifying all our experience. But I cannot quite take the fully realistic view of God, so I ought not to belong to the church.' On the question of *dogmatic theology* we are told: 'The church undoubtedly regards her dogmatic faith as a body of unchangeable saving truths supernaturally revealed to her by God. Now I see the point of Christian dogmatic beliefs when they are at work in the liturgy and so forth, as efficacious symbols of moral change and spiritual growth. But my understanding of the sense in which the church's faith is true falls so far short of the church's own that I don't think I can function in good faith as a fully paid-up member of the church.' And on the question of *ecclesiastical power* they tell us: 'The church is a mighty historical institution, a hierarchy of spiritualized male power that is always, inevitably, coercive, repressive and allied with the haves. But Jesus was one of the poor, a heretic, an outcast and a loser. The contradiction is so overwhelming that until the church turns herself upside-down and actually *becomes* the poor and the heretics, it is more honest to keep clear of her.'

Since around the time of Hegel, liberal theology has been

attempting to meet these entirely reasonable and strongly-felt objections. We have been saying to the honest fellow-travellers: 'Nowadays the church is no longer so rigidly supernaturalist and authoritarian as in the past. You don't have to be a theological realist. You can take a symbolist view of dogma. And the modern church has become humanitarian and does now care for freedom of thought and for the poor. So we truly think a person like you doesn't have to live in self-imposed exile. You can honestly belong to the church.'

This would sound good if the church were willing to back it, but she isn't. Those theologians who confidently assure the world that the church is a reformed character are made to look ridiculous when she repudiates them. Her subtlest punishment is to marginalize them while they are alive and then to falsify them after they are safely dead. The church seems to have decisively rejected liberal theology. It is not wanted. Those liberal theologians who were attempting to coax the exiles back to the church would have avoided a lot of heartache and humiliation for themselves if only they had crossed the floor and joined the exiles instead. Then there would be two distinct phenomena. There would be the visible church, the historic power-structure with its realistic dogmatic faith, and there would be the entirely unorganized invisible church of heretics, artists, writers, humanitarians, lovers of spiritual freedom and of the poor. Nowadays many such people find that they can still usefully associate in certain post-ecclesiastical and non-credal organizations: the great international charities, human-rights pressure-groups and environmental groups. So for Christians who remain able to affirm a full dogmatic faith let there be traditional churches, and for non-dogmatic ethical Christians let there be voluntary work, the caring professions and so forth; and let there be a clear distinction between these two groups. Liberal theology merely muddles things better kept separate.

Does this sound like good sense? It isn't. It is a counsel of despair. It leaves ethical Christianity secularized and cut off from religious community, and it leaves the future of religion tied to that of a conservative church Christianity which is dying very fast. Liberal theology is the church's only hope of a new lease of life, and the only hope of a future for religion.

However, at this point those Christian fellow-travellers who continue in self-imposed exile will wish to intervene. They will say that although they warmly appreciate the way liberal theology has been trying to meet their difficulties, the argument has recently moved on somewhat. Liberal theology now seems to be of the nineteenth century. It is no longer reasonable to claim that there can be a new concordat between our present culture and an appropriately revised Christianity. Things have gone much too far for that. A cultural holocaust has begun in which virtually the whole of our psychic past, philosophical, religious and ethical, is perishing. Nihilism is already rampant. In a sense to be explained, the times are philosophical – and that is why they must be solitaries.

The point of saying that the times are philosophical is this: the difference between theology and philosophy is that you can decently make a career out of theology, but it is slightly grotesque to do so out of philosophy. Theology is typically a profession that serves an institution. It works most straightforwardly in relatively settled times when there is a stable public framework of belief and an agreed vocabulary for discussing ultimate questions. As the early Alexandrian theologians rightly said, religion is the ordinary person's version of philosophy. It is cosmology-plus-philosophy-of-life that has become settled, institutionalized, routinized, made social, political, picturesque and accessible to the public. Religion carries the ordinary person's view of the world and philosophy of life, so that the ideas of almost any kind of thinker can only get across to the public by being placed on the religious map or by having their religious implications spelled out. So true is this that even after three or four centuries of modern physics an Einstein or a Hawking, trying to explain cosmological theory to the public, must still relate it to the ancient biblical picture of an anthropomorphic God creating the world. To this day many folk find that religious ways of thinking come more easily to them than either science or philosophy. Which would be fine – if only we were living in settled times and had a religious vocabulary adequate to our needs. In the service of the church professional theologians might then function as brokers, relating theory in the various sciences to the religious world-view of the public at large. But we are not in such a situation. Society is now so plural, so multifaith and fast-changing and there is such an overwhelming excess of communication that the old common religious world-view is being almost completely replaced by the 'mediascape'. In the media culture theologians disappear and their place is taken by sundry writers, commentators and critics. Religion entirely loses intellectual substance.

The resulting crisis of belief is very extreme. God, the self, the cosmos and objective reality, Meaning, Truth and value have been eaten away, leaving only the mediascape. For the young especially there is nothing but a land of dreams, a flux of images. It is a phenomenalist world of floating personalities in which standardized cues trigger standard bursts of feeling, and whose religion therefore has to be of the contentless charismatic type.

In the mediascape the distinctions between the real and the fictional, the true and the false, the valid and the invalid, real deeds and fantasies – all such distinctions are consumed and lost. Their loss is the loss of reality itself, and the outcome is nihilism, which is a *philosophical* condition. By that I mean that today the old public vocabulary of religion, preaching and theology is bankrupt. Nothing that makes sense can be said in it. That is why nobody takes any notice of it. The correct course of action for a religious thinker is therefore to withdraw from the public sphere (religion, church, theology), in which nothing at the moment can be done well, and to concentrate in seclusion like Heidegger on philosophy. It is because we have no vocabulary and method that we are sure of, and are at a loss, that the times just now are philosophical, calling for the philosophical sort of silent, ruminative waiting out of which alone religious renewal may one day come. Heidegger links this waiting with art in the 1966 *Speigel* interview:

> Philosophy will not be able to effect an immediate transformation of the present condition of the world . . . Only a god can save us. The sole possibility that is left for us is to prepare a readiness, through thinking and poetic creation (*Denken und Dichten*), for the appearance of the god or for the absence of the god in the time of foundering (*Untergang*), for in the face of the god who is absent we founder.

In this way the Christian fellow-traveller who goes into self-imposed exile from the church may be seen as a modern version of a contemplative. But as Iris Murdoch, who has written so much about these characters, makes very clear, *this* contemplative is different. She doesn't retreat deep into the heart of the church. Her austerity is to leave the church and religion behind and to go out into the world and into solitary, anonymous reflection and service. To do this is a symbolic action, a way of bearing unofficial witness to the extremity of the times.[12] And as was suggested earlier, it is hard to make a *profession* out of dedicated unobserved philosophic obscurity.

Yes. But a qualification needs to be added. A certain democratization of philosophy has taken place. I do not mean that members of the general public are reading any more philosophy than they did before, but I do mean that the modern world is very highly reflective, that we are almost all of us aware of the parlous condition of religious language, and that any of us at any time may recoil from the mediascape and wonder what on earth is happening to us and our world. The Heideggerian mood is widespread, and someone like me may be said to have accepted the argument for exile while still remaining within the church. I acknowledge the utter bankruptcy of our received religious and theological language. Apart from what is being done by a handful of ultra-radicals (who almost all live in the English-speaking world, for some reason) there is now no serious new theology. For years I have been able to write theology only out of, and under the stimulus of, French and American philosophy, criticism and social theory. My state of exile is therefore internal rather than external. I bear witness to the strangeness of the times by serving the church from a state of exile within the church, writing theology only out of philosophy. I am an emissary of the world to the church rather than of the church to the world. I am trying to evangelize the church by smuggling into her the faith of the future.

A new denomination?

On the same occasion as the one mentioned earlier, Wittgenstein continued, 'If you feel you must belong to some organization, why don't you join the Quakers?'

But, says Drury, 'The very next morning he came to see me, to say that he had been quite wrong to suggest my becoming a Quaker. I was to forget that he ever mentioned it. "As if nowadays any one organization was better than any other."'[13]

I think this means: 'The times are philosophical, which means

– unsocial and comfortless. We have lost a great deal. But there is no reason either to sit around being romantically gloomy, or to clutch at falsely easy solutions. Be businesslike. Do something honest and ordinary. Look for your own life-path and life-work. Try to make your own tiny bit of truth. Don't for Heaven's sake fall into the ridiculous error of supposing that your problems could be solved by subscription to some suitably abridged Creed or by membership in some cosy, painless group.'

One of my own mentors said to me: 'In other times people like us would have broken away and tried to set up a new denomination.' In other times, he said – but not in these times. There wouldn't be any gain, now. What we have come to recognize about the complexity of religious traditions and the endlessness of interpretation means that we ought to be able to remake our faith and our world by reinterpreting our own inherited vocabulary. At any rate, if we can't do it by bending our own rich native language then we are certainly not going to be able to do it in the thinner and artificial language of some new and smaller group. We should be content to stay where we are. Why not accept the obvious truth that today we have all become so well-informed, and ever so multiple, that we just cannot now expect our allegiances to be as innocent and un-qualified as the allegiances of simpler folk in past times? Modern allegiance is coloured by so much awareness of alternatives that it cannot help but be a little sceptical, questioning and ironical.[14] And a good thing too. Where is the merit nowadays in tribalism or religious fanaticism? Why are we so nostalgic for a childhood world of simple certainties and swift rewards and punishments? More options mean more freedom, more mobility and less bigotry.

What leads people to look for a new denomination is the persisting influence of a deeply-engrained but very harmful assumption widespread in Christian cultures, namely the belief that all the great questions of life will be solved for me if I can but find and commit myself to the right group with the right creed. If I am not happy where I am, I begin to dream that somewhere, somehow, there must be such a group to solve my problems for me. Further, I assume that it is good that faith should be simple, unconditional, unswerving and lifelong. The more doglike we are, the more truth will be vouchsafed to us.

In Christian culture these assumptions created the absolutisms and the cruelties of the past, and they still operate to threaten Europe in particular with fascism. What else can be the political outcome of supposing that real questions can be answered by lordship, corporateness, authority and obedience? When I say the times are philosophical, one of the things I mean is that we have to give up such beliefs. There is nothing such that by surrendering yourself unconditionally to it you can gain absolute truth, security and happiness. Unconditional surrender is just not a good thing at all. Religious truth has to be made or produced by hard ethical and creative work. No group has it ready-made. Just as we need to give up certain objectified and idolatrous notions of God and of the self, so also we should give up the traditional idolatry of the group or the church. Serve her, but with your eyes open.

(c) Conclusion

When we go to church we re-enter a mediaeval universe which, so far as the outside world is concerned, finally passed away over three centuries ago with the spread around Europe of the ideas of René Descartes. The last major literary monuments of the old order in the English language were *The Book of Common Prayer* (1662) and *Paradise Lost* (1667). In these two works something like the world-view of St Augustine is preserved almost intact after twelve-and-a-half centuries. No wonder people are nostalgic for something so archaic, so grand and so enduring. If going to church were the same thing as attending a performance of the York Mystery Plays, reading Dante or visiting a museum of mediaeval art – if, that is, no more were required of us than an imaginative and aesthetic response to a strange and magnificent alien culture – then we would have no problem. Unfortunately the church requires a great deal more of us than that. We are asked to believe that all this stuff is objectively, dogmatically and permanently just True. Furthermore, we are assured that the church's faith is the only true faith. There is no provision for changing it, because it can never be changed. Till the end of historical time being religious will simply coincide with believing all this to be just True. All this is compulsory, forever and immutably.

For at least two centuries liberal theologians have been proposing a revision and modernization of Christianity. The programme was best laid out around the time of the French Revolution and the Romantic Movement by Kant, Hegel and Schleiermacher. It called for a less realistic theism, an end to the supernaturalist world-view, a more experiential and symbolist view of doctrine and a more open and democratic church, purged of the old coercive ideology of hierarchized, spiritualized masculine power.

Unfortunately there wasn't, and perhaps there could not have been, any serious attempt at reform along these lines. Instead we have seen only tokenism. Many senior churchmen assure us most sincerely that they have long taken at least some parts of the liberal programme entirely for granted, but there has been no real change. The layperson going to church still finds the old world-view presupposed by almost everything that is said or sung. The most recent revisions of the liturgy may have moved an inch or two from the older rites, but it takes a specialist to spot the difference. The old doctrinal statements remain in place, and new ones dare not deviate from them by more than a few hairs' breadth. It goes without saying that the old structures of unaccountable, arbitrary power remain in place behind the democratic façades which, here and there, have been hastily thrown up in front of them. Anyone who doubts this may care to investigate what new provision has been made in church law for appeals against unjust rulings or delays by the authorities. None, of course.

The final proof of church tokenism is yet to come. If anything at all of what liberal theology has been saying these past two centuries had really been digested by the church and had been incorporated into her structures, practice and language, then surely a smidgen of it would have got across to the general public? But as we all know, even the most moderate expression of long-established liberal ideas in theology on the part of a bishop is greeted with outrage. Every few years during the twentieth century just the same rather simple ideas about the resurrection or the virgin birth *become unheard-of yet again*. That is to say, some very powerful engine of repression and forgetting must be at work for people to be so unaware that they waxed equally indignant about the same opinions in the last controversy, only a few years earlier.[15] Indeed, the history suggests that members of the Christian public are as rigid and fetishistic in their religious views as those of the Muslim public, and the one religion can no more easily be modernized than the other. The big exception is ethics, to which we will come in a moment; otherwise the hierarchy appear to recognize that so far as doctrine is concerned Christians are like Muslims. The fundamentalist psychology will always be infinitely stronger than liberal arguments. So liberals must be content with tokenism and toleration, because that is all they'll get.

Some journalists and other commentators are inclined to credit Muslim and Christian fundamentalism with intellectual content. One can only surmise that they make this error because they have not read the fundamentalists' writings, which reek of reaction, hysteria and despair. These poor folk know that modernity cannot really be stopped. They know their faith is doomed and their God will die. They have seen the writing on the wall for him, and it has driven them mad. The repressiveness and violence of their response can only accelerate the religious decline that they are trying to arrest. But they are in no mood to listen to the liberals, and for the present their emotions are much stronger than liberal reason. And anyway, the liberals are also too late.

So what are we to do? I have argued that in spite of everything – and we'll get no thanks for it – we should still stay in the church and attempt by deception, by reinterpretation, by political stratagems and by perverting the minds of the young to do something for the transformation of Christianity and the future of religion. We cannot expect to achieve anything by founding a new denomination: who believes in *denominations* any more? Self-imposed exile right outside the church may be the right thing for a very few creative people, but I have suggested that many of us will find it more stimulating to be internal exiles, plotting, scheming and suspected, inside the church. We are not thinking here of the unconscious evasions of the careerists and placemen, but rather of the carefully thought-out deceptions by which we plan to use the old vocabulary as a disguise for smuggling new ways of thinking into the church. We will be deceivers yet true.[16] Since we will never be as strong as the opposition (because we do not believe in that kind of repressive strength) we will instead have to be smarter than they are. That should not be difficult. And there is a case, too, for organized and open dissent. But any organized group of us must not be merely another sect or party with a creed and a cause.

What we seek is a new basis for human association. Religion so far has been based on repression, to a degree which a modern Christian finds utterly incongruous. There *must* be another God than repression. There must be another sort of religious and social strength than strength of repression. Surely there can be a better bond than bondage? The human soul – like the church – is portrayed in Christian symbolism as being feminine. Bearing down upon her is a mighty stack of bigger and bigger masculine figures rising up to the highest Heaven. There's a Father, a Right Reverend Father, a Holy Father, God the Son her Lord and Spouse, and God the Father. And that is a drastically *simplified* version of the ancient system of ecclesiastical and celestial hierarchies which was the ultimate, cosmic, all-male club.[17] It still survives: every major church is still controlled by a small Establishment of middle-aged and elderly men who spend their lives meeting with each other and gossiping about each other, and for whom 'truth' is whatever will keep them – not the church, but them – secure.

Perhaps it is possible to be a Christian feminist *soul*, one for whom all that is just too much, one who wants to see a flatter universe. It is supposed to be a religion of *liberation*, isn't it? Hence we look for a horizontal world in which people are equal but endlessly varied and changing, different from and complementary to each other. The divine-human is realized when I can rejoice in the difference of my equal.

We deferred ethics, but now I return to it. I shall suggest, contrary to our earlier pessimism, that the gradual, unstoppable *ethical* modernization of the churches must eventually destroy Christian doctrine and bring about the triumph of radical theology. The ethical is going to be our Trojan horse.

6

WHAT IS TO BE DONE?

(a) Our Trojan horse

Altizer remarks that in the hands of figures like Dante, Milton and Blake, theology could be as wide as men's vision of the world.[1] But they were lay poets, and that was long ago. Today theology is cut off from the mainstream of culture and is seen as existing to serve the church – which in effect means, the Establishment within the church. In every mainline denomination there is a piece of this Establishment, whose power-base the church is, which has complete control over the church, and which fixes the limits of permissible deviation. It still operates a quietly-efficient kind of censorship of its own: when occasion demands, a consensus can be formed and spread with marvellous speed to the effect that some particular idea is not acceptable. At once, a curtain falls.

This mechanism works so well that it can be relied upon to limit the progress of radical theology within the church for some time yet. It is so good that it even has a saving grace, for in the mainline churches it can and will also exclude fundamentalist and charismatic religion. Those religious styles are populist and anti-intellectual. If they were to penetrate the church Establishment they would take it downmarket, causing it to lose status and to become somewhat less socially and politically consequential. It scarcely needs saying that the Establishment is most sensitive to such matters. Fundamentalist and charismatic religion are therefore *out*. They may be widespread among the inferior clergy and the laity, but they cannot become part of the Establishment. There is a law: the ecclesiastical Establishment can tolerate within its own ranks only that fairly narrow range of views which are compatible with the retention of its own standing with the remainder of the Establishment. Politicians, journalists and others have a very straightforward view of these matters: churchmen should be a little loony but not too much so, a little wet but not too much so, a little idealistic but not so much so as to embarrass others. They should be 'solid' or conservative, and though they may be scholarly they must not be thinkers.

Such constraints may sound trivial, but they matter a great deal. Truth in the churches is political. It is what the Establishment says it is, and what counts as truth for the Establishment is determined by non-theological factors of a social and political kind. Truth is that range of views I must keep within if I am not to forfeit the respect of others, especially other top people. And everybody, but everybody, knows at once who those people are who have transgressed the limits.

There is an irony here. Christian doctrine was defined by the early Establishment, the bishops in the later Roman Empire, in their own interest. The Universe was pictured as being like the Empire itself, a magnificent descending scale of degrees of rank and power, the whole scheme being designed to give the grandest possible cosmic legitimation to the church hierarchy. And as decayed English aristocrats struggle tenaciously to keep the ancestral home in good repair, so you might expect the modern church Establishment to try to maintain what it can of this highly-advantageous system of ideas. Not so: the churches are now relatively open and tolerant, and the traditional instruments for enforcing correct belief lie rusty, long-disused. The Establishment cannot in the old way compel the faithful to remain orthodox, and doesn't even want to do so, because (within the limits already mentioned) its instincts are liberal. But then it is disconcerted to discover that it is not going to be *allowed* to be even moderately liberal in doctrine. On the contrary, external pressures compel it to be rather narrowly orthodox. The public's role-expectations of churchmen confine them within the bounds of naïve doctrinal literalism if they are to avoid causing grave scandal. Bishops are not permitted to be any brighter than the dimmer members of the public.

Once, the bishops told us what to think and burnt us if we did not think it. Today the boot is on the other foot. Politicians, journalists and public opinion tell the bishops what to think, and pillory them unmercifully if they don't think it. This is the media age. The church Establishment quickly grasps the rules of the game, and turns itself into a carefully-selected and self-policing oligarchy with a very limited range of permissible views. There is little choice; in these days the climate of opinion carries all before it.

By a strange paradox however, the omnipresent sovereign power of the media and publicity that works to limit doctrinal change also makes ethics our Trojan horse. For there is nothing that is more completely public and pervasive than the ethical. I have argued elsewhere that everything ethical is manifest, universally-diffused and open to all.[2] The metaphor of a moral *climate*, a common air we all breathe, is just right, because the ethical is carried in and with the language. It is a vast loose-knit system of feelings and valuations annexed to words, and to forms of words linked with practices. It is fully interwoven with language, culture and, indeed, fashion and it evolves all the time with them. You can no more opt out of the ethical than you can opt out of language itself, and in any case the two are inseparable.

Because morality is so important to us, people used to fancy that it must be unchanging, that it must have its own autonomous field of discourse and area of life, and that it must in some way have deep, hidden metaphysical foundations. But in the media age,[3] after having been around for a few decades, one cannot help but recognize that morality is ubiquitous and (strictly) superficial. It is a matter of shifting public sentiment. How often in the past thirty years have we noticed the rapidity with which a new consensus forms and settles!

It does not follow from this that morality is non-rational. (Another platonic prejudice – what is superficial, shifting and of the passions cannot be really important and rational. Rubbish.) But we do need to recognize that ethical argumentation itself also lives and moves wholly inside the shifting manifest realm. We just have to keep reminding ourselves that reason is now altogether inside history. How could it *not* be?[4]

Now I have said that in the modern period – the age of 'the common man' and the common language, that is, the *media* age – the mainline churches are not, and cannot be, fenced off. They are not exclusive sects. They are wide open to the common air. The same winds of language, and therefore of sentiment and of valuation, blow through the churches as through the rest of society. And the church Establishment, which is part of the Establishment generally and is responsive to public opinion, is bound to be influenced by the moral sentiments that prevail in society generally. For example, if a bishop is to retain the respect of a parliamentarian he must as the phrase goes, 'talk the same language', which means that he must feel the same way and therefore share the same valuations. Everyone wishes to know that she or he is sane, is normal, belongs, is one of us; and *sanity is suggestibility*. That is, sanity just consists in being linguistically, and therefore semantically, emotionally and evaluatively fully attuned to others.

It follows that all normal people, including members of the Establishment, are trendy, for such is the nature of language. As language moves it takes us all with it. If we weren't trendy we wouldn't keep together. Of course there are certain psychological differences between conservatives and liberals, and at any one time in society there is a spectrum of prevalent opinions, some more authoritarian and some more relaxed. Games may be played, the conservatives accusing the liberals of liberal trendiness, and the liberals retaliating with counter-accusations of conservative trendiness – but this is all play-acting. In a long historical perspective the common ground among people in the same generation is far greater than their differences. Willy-nilly, we are immersed in our own period and must discuss the ethical agenda that our times set in front of us.

Thus the paradox begins to emerge: the same forces of public and Establishment opinion which in a media age pressure churchmen into being doctrinally conservative *also* ensure that the church is ethically susceptible. As language circulates in the public domain it picks up emotive and evaluative overtones. Inevitably Christians use language in the same way as others, and therefore express the same feelings about the same ethical issues. Feminism is the classic example of a major change in moral sentiment in society at large that simply cannot be stopped from getting into the church, despite the fact that it is profoundly at odds with the doctrinal conservatism which public opinion is also and simultaneously urging upon the church. At the time of writing the Anglican Establishment in Britain has been getting messages from public opinion and the media saying *both* that you must behave like real churchmen *and* that you must concede equal rights to women. These contradictory signals have split the Establishment into factions which are at each other hammer-and-tongs, acting out a Punch and Judy show scripted for them by public opinion.

The cross-currents can create confusion, as is shown by this example: historic Christianity was anti-capitalist. Usury is prohibited in the Old Testament and was attacked by church Councils from the fourth century onwards.[5] Its formal condemnation in the twelfth century was reaffirmed by the early protestants. Rome did not finally give up the struggle against it until the nineteenth century. So anti-capitalism is about as strongly-attested a principle of Christian ethics as you could wish to meet, something which indeed a few people in the 1930s still remembered. Yet today the more 'conservative' a Christian you are the more likely you are to be convinced that anti-capitalism is a bit of left-wing trendiness or godless communism. In this as in other matters, today's conservatives ask for repression but misleadingly call it tradition. They don't for a moment really want traditional moral teachings to be restored and enforced. In their own way they are just as trendy as liberals – and couldn't *not* be so.

The paradox emerges more fully. Despite the rapid statistical decline of the churches, doctrinal traditionalism continues to be in the interests of the church Establishment and is demanded of them by public opinion. But there is to be no reinstatement of the ethical corollaries of traditional doctrine. The church is on all sides expected to endorse a modern, post-Enlightenment ethic of liberalism, democracy, pluralism, human rights and so forth. Society stipulates that church doctrine must be traditional but Christian ethics must be modern, and the two are in conflict.

This conflict makes ethics our Trojan horse, for the new ethic to which the church is committed must in time erode away and destroy her old theology. We are too often anti-Hegelians, reluctant to admit that where the West is now just has to be where Christianity is now. The trend is the only Providence. The church's new ethic just *is* what faith now makes of life and life now makes of faith. So it will win. Naturally the old doctrine will not be formally repudiated. But it will die, as indulgences, the treasury of merit and purgatory have already died. And the radical theology which we have been putting forward this past few years is simply the theological and philosophical counterpart of the church's new ethic. As the old doctrines are quietly put on the back burner, the new theology will step-by-step come forward to take their place. It cannot happen quickly, but it must happen eventually.

At present, though, the contradiction between the old theology and the new ethics is so glaring that it puts people under severe mental strain. Here are just a few examples of the conflict.

1. We take it for granted, we scarcely notice, that the language of liturgy and theology portrays the universe as a totalitarian theocracy – i.e., just the sort of régime one would really *hate* to live under. God has all power and control. He is judge and jury in his own cause, and there is no appeal. He has all the rights and you have none, and indeed Jesus himself reportedly insists that we should not demand but waive our rights. Yet the modern church is ethically committed to criticizing despotic theocracies and to supporting the rule of law, democracy, pluralism and human rights. That is, the modern Christian ethic, like modern society generally, is post-theistic. We worship in one political set-up, but we live in, or at least are battling for, another and quite different one. Worship and ethics point in opposite directions. That is a recipe for madness.

2. Doctrine, prayer and sacramental practice say we are unable to deliver ourselves from our sins, and that the more penitent and humble we are and the lower our self-esteem, the better. But in our pastoral work we know that very low self-esteem is terribly harmful to people. It can make them socially incapable, depressives, victims or criminals. How *can* we be simultaneously encouraging people to think better of themselves in ethics and worse of themselves in religion?

3. Traditional doctrine portrayed God as omnipotent. Human beings were not in the modern sense historical agents. The most we could hope for was to be used by God as his instruments in the execution of his plan. The future was in his control alone. But today if a person prominent in public life takes this idea seriously we are alarmed. Thus in the 1950s Archbishop Fisher of Canterbury said it might be God's will that human history should be brought to an end by the use of nuclear weapons, and in the 1980s President Ronald Reagan was reportedly influenced by

similar ideas. Many Christians were genuinely shocked, because modern Christian ethics emphasizes human historical account-ability. It is now we, not God, who must do something about nuclear weapons, the environment, Third World poverty and similar issues. Ethically, it is no longer acceptable to leave such matters to God. Once again there is a flat contradiction, this time between the quietism of Christian doctrine and the activism of modern Christian ethics.

4. A further development of the same theme is as follows: traditional doctrine moved in a world of God-ordained certain-ties, whereas modern people have to live in a world of humanly-calculated probabilities. Before the Enlightenment the issues of life were in the hands of God. The future was fixed, though we did not know how. 'I will die on 22 May 2004' was either certainly true because that was what God had ordained, *or* it was certainly false because God had ordained otherwise. The world was a real cosmos, and nothing was random. Everything was predetermined. But today the date of my death is a question of probability. That is why life insurance companies are able to operate. We no longer have a fully God-controlled cosmos. The world has become a matter of statistics and chances. Christians, and church bodies, who plan ahead and budget and design presuppose a conception of the universe quite different from that embodied in traditional doctrine and worship.

Incidentally, I once held the fully theistic view of the world. I tried to be consistent, and refused to have any insurance cover. But now that I am not a metaphysical or realistic theist, I am prepared to pay pension contributions. Are you consistent in this matter, and if not, why not?

5. God is infinite in his wisdom and power, and has directly communicated to us a unique and final revelation of saving truth. Christian beliefs are absolutely, immutably and exclusively just True. It follows from these traditional affirmations that all other faiths and points of view are just mistaken, and as the old maxim declared, 'Error has no rights'. Yet today even conservative church leaders are obliged to concede effective parity to the Jews, and to affirm their profound respect for all other major faiths. In our practical dealings with people of other religions no other policy is morally possible. Again there is a contradiction between

the absolutism demanded in theology and the relativism required in ethics.

6. The Bible and Christian doctrine are pervaded by supernatural and messianic beliefs. But when we meet such beliefs in real life we cannot help but see them as pernicious or as symptoms of mental disorder. It is not a good thing for a nation or an individual to be convinced of a special destiny to carry out a unique mission in the world. I don't want people to hear voices or to cast out devils. Increasingly we find the whole psychology of messianism and supernaturalism pathological in ethics and in modern life, although it remains very prominent in the Bible, the liturgy and doctrine.

Religious thought has a proverbial ability to absorb such contradictions, but this is ridiculous. It puts people, and it puts the Faith as a whole, under very severe strain. How did we get into such a mess?

Religion in the West has long been seen as a relation between two terms, God and man. These two terms symbolize two different standpoints from which the religious situation can be viewed. The God's-eye-view is history-transcending, perspective-less and timeless, infinite and absolute. A God-centred theology will be a theology from Above, authoritative and unchanging, with the emphasis on cosmic hierarchy, worship and other-worldly aspiration. In philosophy Plato and Aristotle will be prominent, and in religion the ideal life will be that of the celibate contemplative. Such a God-centred religion predominated throughout the whole mediaeval period from the founding of Constantinople to its fall, or (stretching it a bit) from the fourth century to the seventeenth.

Yet there has always been a minority report.[6] A Christ-centred type of theology looks at religion just from the human end. It says, as Western thought has commonly said since the Enlightenment, that we mortals have available to us only the human point of view, perspectival, inside history and culture, finite and relative. This Christ-centred theology is therefore necessarily a theology from below, occasional, critical, without any special authority and merely of a particular period. It lays the chief stress on historical change, the ethical and our life in the here and now. Religion is just for the sake of our this-worldly life and activity, for we have nothing else. Religion of this type is glad to be *only human*. Its beginnings may be traced back to the mid-seventeenth century, when Descartes founded modern philosophy within the finite human subject, and religion in France turned to a Christ-centred piety. Nearer to us than that is the revolution in philosophy brought about by Kant and Hegel, whose chief long-term effect was to temporalize or enhistorize human reason. Today, those who take the view of religion that I am describing may be followers of Marx or of Wittgenstein, or they may be pragmatists or post-structuralists. There is considerable variety, but the common factors are *a commitment to immanence*, a resolution to stay within the limits of language culture and history and stop pretending we can jump out of space and time; and *a commitment to practice*, that is, a recognition that it is we ourselves who through our social intercourse establish all our meanings and valuations and our view of the world.

All this shows that the conflict within the modern church between the old theology and the new ethics is a conflict between two different religions from two different epochs. People are still very nostalgic for the objective metaphysical God and the eternal world-above of pre-Enlightenment times, so they expect the church to keep alive that ancient vision of the world. But at the same time they also want the church to validate modern reality, that is, to share and endorse all the valuations that together constitute our modern vision of the world. They want the church to reconcile the two Christianities and so reassure them that the new world is not so completely different from the old as might be feared. This contradictory dual demand from the public gen-erates all the controversies that trouble the modern church. And my suggestion is that if we stay with the church and keep quietly pressing the modern viewpoint we may be given a bad time but in the long, long run we must surely prevail.

(b) *The discipline of the Void*

What are we to do about prayer and worship? They seem to make less and less sense to us. Why shouldn't Christianity just give them up?

The suggestion is not as paradoxical as you might think. Consider the environmental movement. It is doctrinally like a religion, for it diagnoses something globally wrong with us and prescribes the only remedy. It detects basic flaws in our assumptions and values and therefore in our institutions, as a result of which we have become locked into an unsustainable way of life. We are heading for destruction. We need a massive conversion of life – and the movement's demand for a complete change of life at the material, economic and social level is arguably grander and more ambitious than the relatively 'spiritual' and individualistic conversions that many other faiths seem content with. At least as much as Islam, the environmental movement aims at a whole new vision of the world with a new economic system and social order. Many-faceted and charismatic, environmentalism is also *structurally* like a young religion still in its early stage of ferment. It has a large literature, campaigning evangelistic organizations, experimental communities, dedicated figures both professional and unpaid, a passionate concern for moral and spiritual values, and a liking for publicity coups, symbols, mascots and issues. What it does *not* need is the fully-developed apparatus of a church, a priesthood and fixed truth. It does better in a fast-changing world to remain fluid and adaptable.

Doctrinally and structurally, then, environmentalism is rather like some religions. Also religious is the way it evokes a special kind of feeling about a greater Whole of which we are part, into which our life is woven and on which we depend. That the ecological vision of the world is both genuinely religious and perhaps destined to emerge as ecclesiastical Christianity's legitimate successor is suggested by such forerunners of it as German Idealist philosophy, Whitehead, Julian Huxley and Teilhard de Chardin. But whether Christianity passes into it or not, the environmental movement indicates what religion may possibly be like in future, after the end of the distinction between the sacred world and the profane. Environmentalism is highly monistic: *only one earth*, it says emphatically. There is nowhere and nothing else for us but this, *so* . . . The vision is very secular, but it is also very religious. Because there is only this, and we have neither anywhere else to look to nor anyone else to pass the buck to, we must look after and care for this earth of ours as diligently as men once served their gods. As for the 'Armageddon' idea that we can quite cheerfully contemplate the destruction of our whole biosphere because God will snatch us safely away to live somewhere else – *that*, to the new religion, is a blasphemy against the earth. And this new nature-religion for which the profane is the sacred does not seem to need prayer or worship. Loving the earth takes their place.

So it is conceivable that Christianity too might become a purely secular humanism without ceasing to be a faith. It could abandon the other-worldly orientation implied by our traditional practices of prayer and worship, turn to the neighbour as environmentalism turns to the earth – and yet still be clearly religious in shape and content.

However, there can be no doubt that for most people in the West private prayer and public worship are central and definitive religious practices. Even to consider giving them up is startling. Why should anyone contemplate such a thing? Because, it is suggested, prayer and worship as ordinarily understood and practised are bound up with a hopelessly-obsolete vision of the world and by now have a great deal wrong with them.

Most people are realists about prayer. In their usage the word meditation is appropriate when we are just thinking by ourselves, whereas prayer is a matter of holding converse with a spirit. The one who prays does so because she wants to express herself to and communicate with a powerful invisible Person who, she thinks, is listening to her. This animistic 'dialogue' conception of prayer is still the norm. It is surprising that modern people should want to think like this. But they do, and since they seem unable to grasp a non-realist notion of prayer,[7] it may even be advisable to try to discourage the practice altogether as harmful. For the problem with person-to-Person dialogue prayer is that the idioms in which it is taught and explained have the effect of discouraging – even forbidding – serious scrutiny or scientific testing of what we are doing. In the absence of reflection and criticism, prayer only too easily degenerates into auto-suggestion or uncontrolled fantasy. Exactly what is there to save it from becoming intellectually dishonest, self-deceiving or manipulative?[8]

As for public worship, non-eucharistic worship in the Western churches is largely derived from the Divine Office of the monks. Sung morning and evening prayers represent a prolongation into the modern world of the monastic ideal. The layperson was seen as a *tertiary*. The noblest life a human being could live was the life of a nun or a monk, a life spent in full-time anticipation of the worship of Heaven, singing the Divine Office. For us who must live in the world, our best chance is to wear the monks' cast-offs. We follow them at a distance, our devotions being borrowed and drastically cut-down versions of theirs.

The one new feature added when the Divine Office of the monks was turned into the Daily Office of the parishes was a heavy dose of royal ideology. Just before the Reformation the Tudor monarchs had already grasped that the church was potentially a very effective publicity machine. When their opportunity came, they naturally made the most of it. Thereafter when the English went to church they were saying yes to the crown, yes to the state and the social order, and a more remote yes to the monks and the mediaeval world view. Mediaeval people looked up to monks and nuns and copied their piety. Today, television news shows us images of the Queen and the Prime Minister attending church. We are supposed to be reassured, and to wish to copy them.

The Reformation had set out to create the first genuinely lay piety, a magnificent ambition. But what did it achieve? It said to the lay person, 'You'll go on worshipping like a monk, only instead of looking up to the heavenly world you'll be taught to look up to your betters in general and to the King in particular.' If you think this verdict one-sided, inspect the interiors of English churches abroad in countries like India or Ireland. They are monuments to the crown, the gentry and the military. It is not surprising that the long-term historical results of all this have been so disappointing. And if the Established Protestant churches of Northern Europe have a particularly dismal record, *all* churches share many of the same problems with worship. It is too other-worldly, too extra-historical and too quietistic. There is a natural suspicion that the great ones who authorized these forms of worship for our use stood to gain by encouraging us to mistrust ourselves, to be apolitical and to look to another world. And in any case, since all human life is lived inside language and society and history, the form of consciousness involved is illusory. Today, lay Christian worship should not purport to be taking place in an antechamber of heaven, a step outside historical time. The point is obvious; and yet the situation is getting worse, not better. *The Book of Common Prayer* (1662) gives a rather vivid impression of the cultural and political world that produced it. Its replacement, the *Alternative Service Book* (1980), floats in a social vacuum, its pages containing no reference anywhere to any of the distinctive features of modern civilization such as democracy, industry, growing knowledge, religious pluralism, feminism and historical change. The book moves in a Heritage limbo, pseudo-traditional and outside real history. In relation to the lives we are actually living and what is making news at the end of the twentieth century, the *ASB* services are the purest fantasy. Morally speaking, we might just as well be spending our time in church reading *The Lord of the Rings*.

The situation with the various Sacraments, occasional offices, rites of passage and so forth is better than it is with the Daily Office. These rites bear more directly upon people's lives, marking or effecting genuine moral changes. They evidently still make a lot of sense to people, for they remain popular. Great efforts have been made over several generations to give the eucharist back to the *laos* and to restore its moral significance.

Impressive, but problems remain. The eucharist continues to invoke an hierarchical vision of the universe and a contrast between the earthly and heavenly altars. In the recitation that opens the Consecration Prayer, the *anaphora*, the biblical salvation-history is inevitably given exclusive, privileged cosmic status, because we cannot yet even *imagine* ourselves being intellectually generous enough to recite a multifaith history of salvation at the Christian eucharist. All Christian rites still privilege just one cultural tradition in a way we know is wrong but haven't the spiritual strength to put right. Further, the exceedingly complex theology of the Great Tradition has long ceased to be understood by the laity or even the clergy. Cultural change and the proliferation of new branches of knowledge have gone so far that the old theological skills cannot be restored. What flourishes is the Lesser Tradition of the Evangelicals, the House Churches, the Charismatics, the Media evangelists and popular Catholicism. It is populist, highly simplified, psychologically manipulative, often very successful – and utterly inaccessible to any reflective person.

A good deal of popular worship is like this. We are going to become American, steeped in undenominational mass religiosity of a sort that wholly excludes intellectuals. In any case, the worst difficulty for us with every form of Christian prayer and worship currently practised needs to be re-emphasized. They are still rooted in the archaic world-view that postulates the reality of powerful invisible spirits. What is archaic is the fact that these beings are somehow always present to our minds, hovering on the margins of consciousness so that they and we belong to each other and can communicate with each other, while yet they are very powerful and easily provoked to wrath, so that we must placate them and seek their favour and protection.

Animism, the spirit-haunted consciousness, appears to be universal in the churches, and no Archbishop or Bishop dare disavow it. A decade ago, hoping not to offend tender susceptibilities, I called it things like 'theological realism' – too kind a label. We should not talk to beings who are not there. We should not believe that there are things like demons, ghosts and spirits.

A modern person ought to be spiritually strong and healthy enough to live and die without superstition. Nothing is hidden. Everything is just what it appears to be and there is no occult reality. The world is ours and there is nothing conspiring against us. There is only the manifest, the world of appearances which is best analysed philosophically as a world of signs. There is only this beginningless endless flux, the human world of doings, meanings and feelings. A Christian is a person who chooses to live in the world as it is, and not, in the C. S. Lewis manner, one who obstinately affirms the superior reality of an imaginary world to which he has retreated. Children's books in the Anglo-Saxon world are written by lonely adults who have had acute difficulty in growing up. Through their books they reach out to other lonely children with stories about how to find a way through to a magical happier world than this. Through many minor writers of this type – George MacDonald, E. Nesbit, Arthur Machen, David Lyndesay, Charles Williams and others now forgotten – a new Anglo-Saxon apologetics of romantic irrationalism developed. Nobody can stop me believing in the supernatural world. The modern world is grey and debased. By protesting against it, I join the poets and affirm the superior power and reality of the world of the creative imagination.

Fine, if you really *are* a strong poet who can make the rules. Fine, if you are a member of the middle classes and someone else is earning and baking your bread while you dream. Fine, if supernaturalism is what above all else you want to save. But disastrous as a recipe for the religion of people who have to live in the middle of life and make a living among others. Gore Vidal has said unkindly that twice-born faith is for people who are content that they and their children should spend their lives 'pickin' cotton'. In British terms, this means that supernaturalism is for the marginalized, the genteel, those who are economically not very active, those who are coming down in the world, those who in one way or another are lonely children.

No doubt such people deserve comfort. But it is not in the long run healthy for the church that they should be so dominant that they virtually have the place to themselves. We also need a Christianity for the middle of life where language circulates fastest and for the vigorous economically-active people who have no need or time to retreat into inwardness. These people have no insides. They simply live in the real world. What you see of them is all there is. They do not need to dream. They are the sanest ones, and they support the rest. They deserve a religion too, and it cannot any longer be animistic. It cannot invoke hidden beings or any supernatural world. It will have to be a religion of the brightly-lit foreground in the middle of life and language, and not of the margins or the background.

Unexpectedly perhaps, I am calling this religion for the middle of life 'the discipline of the Void'. The point of the phrase needs to be explained at once.

First, a number of modern theologians led by John Robinson have simply *equated* the religious realm with the realm of human interpersonal relationships. To pray is, and is only, to give oneself unconditionally to a fellow human being. So God or the religious realm is just a quality of whole-heartedness or generosity in giving oneself to others. It is *disponibilité*, being for others. But this ecstatic anthropolatry is not what we teach. In fact, we are very wary of it. There's nothing but the human world, but it does not follow that one should worship the human absolutely.

On the other hand, by the discipline of the Void I do not mean that the human realm as it were floats in endless empty Space and that we ought to spend a lot of our time ruminating on this encompassing vacuity. Some of the language used by Edward Craig, as he writes about William James, seems to be painting a picture of this type. Humanist philosophy, he says for example, involves a 'metaphysical vision of the autonomous agent in the void', and the void 'starts just beyond our sense-experience'.[9] I don't want to put forward quite this view because I fear that the metaphors involved will not be effective for much longer. Outside the human realm there is nothing, not even nothingness, because the human realm is outsideless. It has no 'beyond'. So there is no Void out there. The feeling of nothingness is just a feeling of nostalgia for the lost metaphysical support of our life. But the loss was not a real loss; it was only the loss of an illusion. After it is dispelled no hole or gap is left where it used to be. In due course the feeling of loss will itself be lost. In the Southern hemisphere we no longer feel liable to fall off the earth, because we have forgotten the theories that suggested we might. Dead theories may leave a feeling of nostalgia behind them for a while, but eventually they are forgotten, and then the nostalgia goes.

Similarly, I suggest that before long people will just lose the feeling of being metaphysically unsupported and will therefore no longer call up the image of being surrounded by nothingness. So do not, please, read me as making a god of the gap left by the death of God. That is the last and most ingenious God of the gaps – the God of the god-shaped blank left when realistic belief in God is lost. But that is not what I am teaching. Rather, for me the Void is what in Buddhism is called emptiness, nothingness or Sunyata.[10] It is not an additional blank region beyond life and surrounding life, but rather is the experienced character of our life itself. It is the poignant insubstantiality, fleetingness or contingency of everything. It is life's own strange fusion of endlessness and transience. On the one hand we pass through life only once, with no retakes. Our freedom and the only-once-ness of life thus creates an awesome sense of the utter finality and solemnity of life, while yet on the other hand we also see that our life is unobserved and gratuitous, without basis or goal. It has no ground, we are not responsible to anyone and we are not going anywhere. And this thought makes our life seem to us unbearably slight and unimportant.

As Western thought this last hundred years has gravitated or rather levitated irresistibly towards nihilism, so we have come to experience the Void as a pervading nothingness-in-the-midst-of-life. And I am arguing that piety for us should in future take the form of a Discipline of the Void. That is, I am not advocating a purely humanist religion, an idolatry of the human. And I am not advocating a religion directed towards a supposed metaphysical

Void that surrounds human life. I am not even advocating a nature religion that worships or celebrates biological life itself. But I am advocating a religion of life in the sense of a spiritual discipline that enables us to accept and to say yes to our life as it is, baseless, brief, pointless and utterly contingent, and yet in its very nihility beautiful, ethically-demanding, solemn and final.

You may say that this is Buddhist and not Christian. Now I have no desire whatever to dissociate myself from Buddhism; it is rather an honour for a Westerner to be thought to deserve that name. But however that may be, something very close to what I have in mind is in fact to be found in the Christian philosopher Kierkegaard. As everybody knows, Kierkegaard was a determined opponent of Hegel's attempt to exhibit all of history as the unfolding of a rational scheme. According to Kierkegaard, 'Nothing ever comes into existence with necessity . . . All coming into existence takes place with freedom, not by necessity.'[11] Hegel's philosophy looked towards the past, arguing that because the past is fixed it must be necessary, and therefore the entire unfolding historical process is ultimately necessary. But, says Kierkegaard, the past 'proved by coming into existence that it was not necessary'.[12] If the past had become necessary, it would follow that in some hidden way the future is necessary too. 'If necessity could gain a foothold at a single point, there would no longer be any distinguishing between the past and the future. To presume to predict the future . . . and to presume to understand the necessity of the past are one and the same thing . . .'[13]

The aim of Kierkegaard's discussion is to exorcize necessity from history. He does not deny ordinary causal relations,[14] but will not allow them to become the starting-point for an argument that purports to demonstrate an all-pervading immanent necessitation in history. In an almost Anglo-Saxon manner, Kierkegaard entirely separates the realm of the necessary from the realm of the existent or the historical. The upshot is that the whole of our life-world in every part of it is a sphere of contingency, and therefore of radical uncertainty, and therefore of freedom, and therefore of faith (Tro, belief). When the historian contemplates the past, it should not be with the intellectual satisfaction of one who follows a deduction, but with 'the emotion which is the passionate sense for coming into existence: wonder'.[15] So Kierkegaard begins to import religious attitudes and concepts into the secular realm. Every event in the world, being a coming-into-existence, is uncertain, contingent, elusive and must be waited-upon.[16] On one side of it is the antecedent non-being, and on the other side of it is the purely contingent fact that it was this possibility and not some other that happened to get itself actualized.[17] And what, asks Kierkegaard, is the proper organ of knowledge for a world thus characterized, a world radically contingent, a world of freedom? He answers, *faith*[18] – and so for perhaps the first time in the history of Christian thought goes all out to make the proper place and sphere of faith the sheerly-contingent, uncertain, gratuitous, open-textured life-world itself. This is the first truly protestant and secular faith. It cannot get hold of God himself, for God is other, the Unknown, the absolutely different, with no mark by which it could be distinguished.[19] If it is to find God, faith must find him only within the sphere of finitude: that is all it can handle. So it is no longer directed towards the timeless certainties of the heavenly world above. Like God himself, it has come down to earth.

Faith in consequence is active. 'Belief is a sense for coming into existence . . . the conclusion of belief is not so much a conclusion as a resolution . . . belief is not a form of knowledge, but a free act, an expression of will.'[20] Faith is the overcoming of nihilism: 'It believes the fact of coming into existence, and has thus succeeded in overcoming within itself the uncertainty that corresponds to the nothingness of the antecedent non-being.' And how can faith conquer nihilism: what is going to make a genuinely worldly, lay and protestant religion possible? Answer, the absolute paradox, the astounding idea that God has become just a historical contingency, something as accidental and gratuitous as me. Kierkegaard even goes so far as to say that the objective metaphysical God, God in his eternal reality, is not a proper object of faith. 'Socrates did not have faith that the God existed. What he knew about the God he arrived at by way of Recollection.'[21] That is, the Greek God is *a priori*, an ideal, a mere essence; and 'faith does not have to do with essence, but with being (historical existence).'[22] So the distinctively Christian teaching is this: whereas the philosophical tradition sought an ideal but satisfyingly-rational world above, or even claimed that our own historical world is an expression of Reason, the Christian by faith chooses this life in all its objective uncertainty, its utter contingency, its nihility, and says Yes to it. Christ, because he is God's having become a mere contingency and uncertainty and nothingness, symbolizes the impossible thing that the Christian believes and does. Christ is the bridge across which Kierkegaard brings faith down to earth, making its only proper sphere and field of operation *this* world and not some other.

A century and a half later, I want to go a little further than Kierkegaard. He was battling against a philosophical rationalism that claimed to be able to comprehend the whole of life and faith completely. Hegel had been able to put forward that grandiose claim with some confidence and even plausibility. Our situation is the opposite. Our century pinned its hopes on political ideologies and on scientific and technical rationality, but far from solving the problems of life they have exacerbated them and have worsened our position. So whereas in Kierkegaard's time faith confronted an overweeningly confident rationalism, in our age the issue is nihilism. And by speaking of the discipline of the Void as the prayer of the future, I want to suggest that the 'nothingness' of our life is not to be denied, conquered or escaped from. We should make a friend of it, wait on it. Kierkegaard suggests to us that in Christianity God has entered our life-world and equated himself with its insubstantiality and transience. He has come into being. He is a mere contingent particular. The Word has become flesh, so that the fleshy, the corruptible, the transient is now the religious object.

I am trying to suggest that the early Kierkegaard's extreme incarnationalism brings him unexpectedly close to a kind of world-affirming Buddhism. To say a paradoxical, intense and heartfelt Yes to divinity-in-transience is not very far from clinging to the Void. When Kierkegaard (or his pseudonym Johannes Climacus) defines faith as 'objective uncertainty'[23] he is not espousing a banal agnosticism. He is saying that the believer inwardly and passionately clings to and affirms something absurd that fuses together everything Plato disjoined: the Eternal comes to be, the Universal is a particular, and so forth. We find eternal joy in emptiness, we say an everlasting Yes to the flux. *That* is our worship.

(c) *Ethics after the end of history*

The claim that we live at, near or even after the end of history has often been made in our tradition. It was originally a messianic idea, with a whole complex theology behind it. God is the Lord of history, so that the entire world-historical process unrolls to fulfil a single divine purpose, now approaching its long-awaited fruition. We cannot of ourselves do anything to hasten this event. We cannot even be adequately prepared for it. But we believe and hope that God in his mercy will 'give us the condition'. If we but wait penitently upon him, he will carry us through the fires of his own Judgment. This saving event, due to happen in time, will be the End of time. It has been long, too long, deferred. Its deferral has been history – a period of grace, an interim during which we have been praying *Thy Kingdom Come*. For many a long year we have been expecting and yearning and purifying ourselves, we have been labouring to build up the church and spread the faith, and all in preparation for the great longed-for Event that is going to justify everything. Is it coming now?

It is important to stress the pivotal role of the Parousia or last event, especially in Protestant theology. The End-event bears the whole burden of finally justifying God, his Providence, the entire world-historical process, our faith, our patient waiting and our moral action. Yet this event on which everything depends is right out of our control. We cannot hasten it. We are entirely passive. When it feels close we are filled with ardent, joyous expectation, but when it seems to be receding in a kind of infinite postponement we can suffer from very acute melancholy and pessimism.[24]

In the messianic philosophy of history, then, the claim that we live near the end is the claim that the great longed-for culminating Event that will finally justify everything – justify our faith, all our waiting and our moral striving – is now close. Until it comes we are in darkness. When it has come, all is light. And this conception of history, transposed into a variety of political ideologies and philosophies, has pervasively influenced the Western tradition. Elements of optimistic messianism are traceable in, for example, both Marx and Nietzsche. By contrast, the heartsickness and melancholia of messianic hopes too severely disappointed characterizes the later thought of Adorno and Heidegger.

An important additional feature of messianism and its secular variants is that the whole of human history is seen as a period of probation. We live in a great disciplinary institution, subject to a code of conduct and passing through a series of stages of instruction. 'The Law was our schoolmaster to bring us to Christ',[25] says St Paul. Reaching the End of history is always seen as being like coming of age, completing a journey, or graduating from school and being liberated from institutional confinement and external control. Before the End religion is heteronomous; after it religion becomes autonomous.

Now when today Jean Baudrillard and others say that we live after the end of history they are *not* saying that we suffer from disappointed messianic hopes. They are saying that we have suffered the profounder disappointment of losing the whole complex of messianic ideas. From messianism we got our sense of history as a finite time ahead, a period of suspenseful waiting and striving, looking to a future that will make all our present labours, yearnings and sufferings worthwhile. Losing messianism, we lose the point of life as we have so far understood it. Just as Nietzsche said that not even the supposed atheists had yet understood what the death of God means, so Baudrillard wants us to see what a great event is the end of history as we have known it.[26]

How has all this happened? In the early 1920s, the last great period of messianism, the old European order was felt to be utterly decayed and discredited, and many of the ablest spirits dreamt of rebirth and a 'New Man'. What we got was fascism and communism. Great thinkers who had unwisely pinned their hopes on one or other of these movements suffered severe consequent damage to their reputations. The very idea of rebirth, and every kind of political messianism, is now sunk. In the late 1980s even the Russians and the Chinese are giving it up. It is as if our political development has ended. We cannot now see beyond what we've got, namely the rule of law, human rights and something like liberal democracy. Cosmetic improvements, per- haps – but mostly, a holding operation is all we can foresee. The discrediting of messianism has left us feeling there's nowhere to go. Even gradualist hopes of piecemeal improvement are proble- matic, for if the whole of our life is lived within the ever-shifting relativities of language and culture we can have no unclouded vision of any permanent history-transcending benchmark against which to measure some bit of supposed progress. Imagine an astronaut floating in space who makes cycling movements with his legs: with no background, there's no way of telling whether he's moving or just running on the spot. Something's progress can be detected only in relation to something else that is fixed. But if the notion of progress dies, what happens to history and to moral and political action? We seem delivered over to those futile disputes between people who think the world is getting better and others who say it is getting worse; between those who say moral standards are declining and those who say that on the contrary they are rising. Without any stable background against which to assess such opinions and disputes, we don't know what to do but yawn. The opinions are meaningless, and the disputes therefore interminable.

Not only in politics, but more generally in ethics, epistemology and the doctrine of reason we may well feel that the end of the traditional belief in a Telos or Goal of history threatens us with passivity and stagnation. So the best we can do, many people say, is to be candid. Yes, all is fiction. Yes, there is no progress because there is no fixed and independent criterion to measure it by. And *therefore* we cannot do better than prop up in perpetuity the familiar Enlightenment fictions that are the best myths we've got. Let us then cling obstinately to our old irrational belief in Reason. Let us go on affirming that knowledge is a good thing, that it can be progressively increased to the general benefit, and that we can all come to understand our world and each other better. We need our vague and fuzzy faith that a text has just one original and right meaning. Truth is our best illusion. Hundreds of crusty old academics rant away at us,[27] saying that it is our moral duty to cling to the fictions of the Enlightenment, and of course we must warmly agree with them. It is true that the Enlightenment doctrines are the best fictions we have got. All I am pointing out is that when we say this we are in danger of slipping down helplessly into a vortex of reflexive paradoxicality. As a strategy, holding on to the Enlightenment is not without difficulties. We may become completely paralysed by the scepticism of our rationalism.

Paradox arises in other ways, too. On the one hand we may feel that the failure of the messianic politics of fascism and communism throws us back willy-nilly upon a now-dubiously-rational reaffirmation of Enlightenment ideology. Knowledge, freedom, gradual improvement, liberal democracy. But on the other hand there are grounds for thinking that no moral *tour de force* can keep the Enlightenment belief in progressive improvement going anyway. It is ceasing to be tenable, even as a useful fiction. For a number of our natural sciences, and a number of aspects of our technical and economic development, are fast approaching the limits of what is affordable or of what is environmentally sustainable. Just the cost of developing the next generation of weapons, or of pushing particle physics down to the next level of refinement, gets to be too high. War and big science price themselves out of the market. Something of this sort is happening already in many areas of technology, including some where postmodern taste inclines to prefer a relaunch of the past, anyway. And more generally, as everyone knows, we must limit our numbers, our consumption of non-renewable resources and the environmental impact of our activities, and make the transition to stability. This will end linear historical time, even in its reduced role as a valuable cultural fiction. We won't be *getting anywhere* any longer.

Again, there are also numerous cultural signs of the end of history. Once we had fully developed the historical consciousness by the end of the eighteenth century we were sooner or later going to find ourselves endlessly reviving and parodying all previous historical styles. Revivalism as such is not new: the Renaissance was a classical revival, and John Cosin at Brancepeth, Durham romantically and remarkably revived the glories of the high Gothic in about 1630, almost before it was dead. But our modern revivalism is more extreme than that. It is all we are capable of. We have become so reflective that we seem to have lost the capacity to build a new religion or culture. We know we need a new religion, and a new culture. But we are too ironical. We simply cannot muster that slightly pompous, stuffed-shirt conviction about ourselves which the Victorians still had in such generous measure, and which we would need in order to build a new religion or culture. Perhaps the problem is that a *culture* calls for a higher degree of unconscious solidarity than we have any longer. Irony about what we've got seems all we are capable of. We are trapped by too much historical consciousness. We feel it has all been done before. It is not surprising that High Modernism ran out of steam by the end of the 1920s.

All these factors have been compounded since the end of World War Two by cheap mass travel and the ubiquitous influence of the media. The media have replaced the old political economy, based on social discipline and labour, with a new libidinal economy[28] in which media images shape and direct our desires. Mass communications, the libidinal economy and mass tourism are together bringing about the rapid worldwide dissolution of all traditional religious and cultural identity and its replacement by a flux of libidinally-charged images of products and personalities, the 'mediascape', with its correlate, an empty and anonymous type of human being. Further, the media scatter reality by broadcasting events indiscriminately, and immeasurably far beyond their normal range of causal impact. This means that the secondary media reporting of an event is a much more powerful occurrence than the original event itself. This in turn means that media reality becomes 'hyperreal', more potent and more real than ordinary reality.[29] Though dead at the level of ordinary reality, Humphrey Bogart is immortal in hyperreality. Part of the consciousness of more than a billion people, he transcends the ordinary limits of time and space and is a lot more real than you or me. At any one time he will be appearing somewhere, usually to millions. And this hyperreality of everything in the mediascape has undermined our notions of the shape and limits of moral and political action, leaving us uncertain of how any longer to distinguish between the real and the fictional, between the important and the unimportant, between what I must react to and what I may disregard, between genuine political action and mere media manipulation, between what happens only in the media world and what takes place in the 'real' world.

For example, I subscribe to Greenpeace. Is it a public-relations or lobbying organization whose activities consist solely of media stunts, or is it doing real things for the environment in the real world? I don't know and they don't know, because there isn't any workable distinction between the two any more. Isn't it as if history as orderly narrative is getting replaced by an endless irregular flurry of stage-managed media events jostling for attention? Many of the most prominent public figures spend much of the day not acting, but acting for the cameras, for they know that nowadays the *real* event is not the event but the media report of the event. And the media disturb our sense of reality not only by blurring reality and fiction, action and playacting, and not only by disrupting causality and scattering events; they also confuse us by their distinctively cavalier attitude to time. Is what we see 'real' or a later restaging, photographed or faked, live or recorded, in 'real time' or not? Often, we don't enquire about the status of what we see. We don't bother to place the timescale, and don't bother about truth or fiction. At the very bottom of the market in Britain and the USA there are now newspapers that publish science fiction as news. Who cares? The stars began all this by living in a hyperreal timeless present, media eternity. As we enter the fully developed museum culture in which everything is limitlessly recorded, stored, retrieved and replayed, different figures, events and periods real and fictional become just a range of aesthetic options all equally real and endlessly available in a continuous present. The contemporary 'real' world is merely one of several options, and not necessarily the most attractive of them.

It is considerations such as these that prompt people to say that *les grands récits*, the great mythic legitimating narratives of the West have broken down.[30] 'Reality' itself is breaking down; hence non-realism. Even worse, our ideas of the formation and the continuity of the moral personality and of moral intention, action and desert are breaking down. We are losing our sense of a unique, enduring, responsible moral identity being formed once for all as it makes its way through irreversible linear time. That particular sort of protestant ethical selfhood is disappearing, melting away.

There is a domino effect at work. The end of political and religious messianism knocks over all belief in a grand Telos or Goal of history. Down then goes linear time, and next the pilgrim view of life as a journey. The moral unity and coherence of our life – in a word, the solid moral *self* – is the next to fall . . . how much more of this is there going to be?

Just at present the issue is moral action. Our difficulty is that Western thinking has been highly instrumentalist. The legacy of the hierarchized theistic universe of the past is that we still have difficulty in seeing a particular act as being intrinsically worthwhile just in its own local context. Everything I do has got to please someone higher up, or has got to fit into some larger context, or has got to serve some greater purpose or conform to some general rule, or has to be instrumental in achieving some more ultimate goal. This instrumentalism or utilitarianism has its background in the mediaeval cosmic and social order, and yet it has also made us good capitalists and scientists. Our motives are always *ulterior*, that is, we are looking *beyond*. Everything needs to justify itself in the face of and to be explained in terms of something larger and higher, more general and rational than itself. In history it is as if every note struck must make just the right contribution towards the build-up of the final crescendo. Only God is for his own sake, and everything else is for God's sake. So everything has to look to its own finalization in God and God alone.

The assumptions beyond this moral instrumentalism are twofold. First, it is very important to be a unified self who lives a unified life, for the whole world-process just does eventually unify everything in God. Secondly, we have been created eccentric, in the strict sense that our centre of gravity lies outside us. The unifying principle around which our lives must be focussed and towards which our every act must ultimately be oriented is God. But 'God' is a queer vague word. Here it signifies not just the metaphysical Ground of the world but also the Telos, the Goal of history, the 'chief End of Man', the future consummation of things, that towards which we look forward in hope and expectation. The linguistic idioms and the images of God are so diverse, complex and puzzling that they obviously cannot be understood realistically – but we need not revive *that* dispute here. All we need point out here is that the idioms and images are designed to hammer home two of the central doctrines of the West: our life needs to be ethically unified, and it has to be unified eccentrically. It finds the unifying Ground, the justifying Goal, and the ultimate focus of moral aspiration that it has got to have by looking Ahead. That promised glory and goal Ahead is seen by Westerners as alone making our life meaningful, because it makes of our life a journey with a destination, or a narrative with a conclusion. Similarly at the public and social level: history is a meaningful story insofar as it is going somewhere and the future can be confidently expected to justify the past.

So the moral life needs to be unified, it needs to be unified eccentrically, and both for the individual and for society as a whole the great Focus of this eccentric unification lies Ahead. These doctrines make life make sense because they picture our life as being written like a book. The world has a plot. We are getting somewhere. In the last chapter all the loose ends will be tied up. Everything will be totalized, unified and justified in God.

No, it won't: we just lost all that. Did not Jewish messianic hopes perish in the gas-ovens of the Shoah? If by a 'point' to life people mean a future Telos, a promised focus, goal and reward that will reconcile, fulfil, explain, justify and consummate everything – then life now has no such point. There is going to be too much left over that is unjustified and unjustifiable. An ethically satisfactory totalization of this history of ours is just unthinkable. It is all too much of a mixed bag. The story doesn't get rounded off. We all just peter out inconclusively.

The result in Western eyes is nihilism, because the notion that our life's point and justification have got to be final and extrinsic is so deeply engrained in our tradition. For most people religion, and for many people morality, just *is* the belief that what's within the horizon of our life derives all its value from something else beyond the horizon. We are all like a young couple with a mountain of debt, slaving away to pay off their premiums, instalments and mortgages in order to gain a hypothetical security decades ahead. Almost our whole life, our whole culture, has been ulteriority (instrumentalism, utilitarianism). When that extrinsic Last End of all our action is lost, it seems that life is pointless.

At one level, the remedy is obvious. It is what anybody will tell you: we need to get life's centre of gravity back into the centre of life, and so to reunite life with itself. We have to take life as it comes, making the most of it from moment to moment and from day to day. Robert Graves made the point by holding up a bunch of grapes by the stalk, so that it hung down as it does on the vine. 'Now', he would say, 'If you eat the bunch grape by grape from the top down you'll find that at each moment the next grape will be the very best of all the ones you have left. That is how we should live.' Neat; but it is not religion or morality. It is just pagan passive aestheticism, and it is the merest cliché. It changes nothing. Nothing indeed *can* change until we overcome the philosophical and institutional conditions that keep on producing the ulteriority which, when disappointed, turns into nihilism.

Once again, if we dig deep enough we get down to sexism. Morality, that is, the bourgeois-industrial morality of masculine planning, discipline and control, is ulteriority and ulteriority is yet another facet of sexism. This time woman is to man as present is to future. Woman represents the value-claims of present sensuous immediacy whereas man represents the rational principle that requires us to forgo short-term satisfactions and organize our efforts towards the attainment of a larger and more unified long-term good. Thus the subjection of woman is a visible enactment of the triumph of morality-as-ulteriority:

woman	man
present	future
short-term	long-term
intrinsic	instrumental
immediate satisfactions	deferred satisfaction
the passions	reason
plurality	unity
body	soul
nature	spirit

In the protestant cultures of the past three or four centuries there is an obvious and much-discussed connection between sexism, long-termism, the dominance of masculine reason and the emergence of science-based industrial capitalist society.[31] Masculine reason consciously distances itself from and seeks to control everything that is immediate, volatile, female, emotional and natural. It impersonalizes itself, becoming general and detached. Then it plans, legislates and organizes. Historically, technological rationality is without doubt the legatee of the old Greek distinctions between reason and the passions, form and matter. From Plato's *Timaeus*,[32] from Aristotle *On the Generation of Animals* and from other Greek texts it appears that these distinctions are indeed sexist in origin. Sexism, that is, provided the metaphoric that made it possible first to formulate the distinctions between reason and the passions, form and matter, particular, changing sensuous immediacy and long-term rational control by principles – the distinctions upon which modern culture still depends.

However, it does not follow that modern science must remain sexist. It does not have to continue striving to deliver 'more bang for your buck'. There is an ever-increasing number of women scientists, and in our future development we may very well turn (and *have* to turn) towards biology, communication and a stable, interwoven, nurturing relationship between the world of culture and the world of nature. The objectification and subjugation of nature must stop and be replaced by the full adoption of nature into culture. During the past thirty years this has already begun to happen. French philosophy and Anglo-Saxon philosophy of science have adopted and incorporated nature into culture, so that nature is no longer a wild thing outdoors but is inside and part of the human household. At a more everyday level, environmentalism has the same effect. The whole globe becomes a farm.

These developments are more hopeful than popular anti-science, and (with a bit of luck) they will make obsolete Heidegger's pessimism about technological rationality. Some-what as in Plato's myth the emergence of the two sexes, male and female, represented a fall from the original perfection of the Androgyne, so Heidegger suggests that the very making of the form-matter distinction at the beginning of Western thought was sinful because it ruptured the primal unity of Being.[33] Originally Being had simply 'presenced' or communicated itself to us. That was how it should be. But the philosophers were not content with this. They set up an intelligible order of Forms somehow prior to and above Being, in order to subject Being to the control of thought – and by describing the issue in this way Heidegger portrayed the whole of Western thought (and in particular, scientific and technical thinking) as fallen almost from the very beginning, and trapped himself in an ultra-Lutheran pessimism and quietism from which there could be no deliverance except by a *deus ex machina*.

I am suggesting, however, that we do not need to be anti-science. Nor does science have to be above the law, privileged and exempt from criticism. We can demythologize it, see it as a cultural activity, expose its concealed assumptions and aims and, if necessary, redirect its course. Science does not have to be sexist, exploitative, power-hungry and allied with the military. It can be redirected. Nor does it have to be our only, or our dominant, way of thinking. Other and different ways of thinking can be brought in to counterbalance it.

We got into difficulties at this point because metaphysical monotheism led us to believe in the totalization of knowledge. Ultimately, we have thought, there must be just one great system of absolute knowledge and one ruling set of intellectual standards. From the theologians who preceded them the scientists tended to inherit the conviction that in the end there is only one Truth and they as a group hold the key to it. So they claim something like benefit of clergy: they have a right to the presumption that their activities are valuable and their motives uncorrupt. They have a right to privileged status and public funding. They have a right to be the standard by which the intellectual respectability and the social value of all other people's activities are judged. Because the culture has remained at heart monotheistic the scientists inevitably became a new monopolistic priesthood, and so in due course attracted a new sort of 'anticlerical' hostility against themselves.

Radical Christians, however, are pluralists. We don't believe in an objective absolute Unity of either God or Truth or the human soul. We think all three are now dispersed, plural and multifarious. Nobody should be exempt from criticism and there doesn't need to be any Queen of the Sciences, whether theology or physics. We don't want to privilege *anything*. We don't want to privilege the unity of our own souls and the quest for personal holiness and personal salvation. We don't want to privilege either the unity of Truth, or any particular way to truth. We don't even want to privilege any particular notion of God. The traditionalist outlook, being chiefly interested in social control and the maintenance of tradition, liked to portray Truth as One, unchanging and to be gratefully received by us. But radical Christians are non-realists and expressivists. We see truths *in the plural* as continuously produced by human creative activity, like art, as we go out of ourselves and into communication. Truth is social. It is not timeless, solitary and pre-existent. Like life and love, it is temporal, public, ambiguous, ever-changing and ever-renewed. Truth is not One, it is many. It is known not by those who keep themselves to themselves, but by those who communicate themselves.

Because we are non-realists we can take a cheerfully pragmatic view of science and its intellectual pre-conditions. It doesn't frighten us. We are quite happy to make pragmatic use of the form-matter and fact-value distinctions in our science and technology and we are quite happy to be ulterior in matters of industrial and social planning, without becoming the slaves of those ways of thinking. Indeed, our religion, morality and art will be consciously corrective. They will set out to counteract, and to liberate us from, the ways we must think in our science, technology and administration. By all means let us look at a sunset with the eyes of a physicist when it is appropriate to do so, but as a corrective let us learn also to look at a sunset with the eyes of Turner. We must learn to be plural, Japanese and Zen. Pragmatically we'll certainly need to learn the intellectual skills of the scientist and the manager: analysis, testing, optimization, forward planning. But we will not fetishize the ways of thinking involved so that they alienate us from life and rob the immediate 'this, here' of value.

Of course any future culture must continue to be based on science and technology. There is no choice about that: we will need very tight management and many new technologies, if we are to make ever-more-efficient use of diminishing resources while also remedying some of the worst environmental damage already done.

Big science has for generations been organized in a distinctly hierarchical and indeed paternalistic way. But the new information technologies store, retrieve, process and circulate information so effectively and cheaply that they make great concentrations and hierarchies of power unnecessary. Society no longer needs to be a pyramid. It can be a horizontal network, a pulsing multicellular organism, and still be efficient.

Technology and administration in various ways require us to split and devalue Being by thinking of things instrumentally and in terms of control. We divide form and matter, theory and experience, reason and the passions, fact and value, proximate and remote, means and ends and so on. Our religion will cultivate a wisdom that undoes these distinctions in a spiritual movement of reconciliation. Life is fully returned to itself. Value flows back in. Being in all its plenitude is experienced in the fleeting instant.

Our religion, then, will be a training in contemplative wisdom that teaches us how to look at the world in a truly religious way. It will be a post-historical vision, in that it does not look to any future vindication but rather itself vindicates everything right now. Nor are we talking about anything that is in the least esoteric. On the contrary it is something that every artist, every mystical tradition, and every great faith already knows. If our perception of the world has indeed been damaged by too much media bombardment, too much information or too much technological rationality, then it is time for us to invent new kinds of retreat. The musty, manipulative neo-Jesuit style of retreat should in any case have been abolished long ago. We need something more wholesome and more directly related to modern spiritual needs. We should not spend time picking at the scabs on our own souls. We should be training our senses, praying with our eyes open and learning to see the world whole. We don't need introspective retreats; we need art-retreats and nature-retreats.

Our ethic, similarly, will be extravertive or world-directed. We will spread out and try to revalue as many classes of people, aspects of life and bits of the world as we can. If it is the case that instrumental ways of thinking and media bombardment have deadened our senses and devalued life, then for us the religious task is the creation of intrinsic value – and because we are not moral realists, it makes sense to talk of our doing that. I don't see morality as a matter of obeying or conforming to antecedently-existing moral realities. Things have the value we give them; their value is a matter of how much we care about them. We *make* things valuable when we love them generously, disinterestedly and creatively, in such a way as to make their value public.[34] This activity doesn't need external validation. It is morality raised to the level of religion.

(d) The conquest of nihilism

A line of thought going back at least to Nietzsche, and perhaps even to the 1830s and certain of the Romantics, suggests that the death of God must be followed by a crisis of nihilism. The death of God is a complex cultural event. Among other things, it includes the general realization that the world does not get 'totalized': there is no unifying principle, no transcendent focus around which everything converges, no coping-stone that holds everything together. There is nothing that says our life *has* to make sense. There is no moral world-order, no objective purposefulness out there prior to us. Our life has no preset goal, no objectively-given point or meaning. All this, however, seems to deprive our life of moral substance or weight, and since realism is in part at least a feeling of being objectively constrained and morally backed-up, the death of God threatens to erode all that has hitherto given people their sense of reality. The world is no longer a coherent cosmos apart from what we do to make it one for ourselves. As a result the entire onus now falls upon us. We have got to make chaos into cosmos, we have got to create morality, we've got to invent religion as well as art, and we've got to make our own lives meaningful.

Of course we don't have to do all this for ourselves, from nothing. You and I and everyone else have all inherited a cultural system evolved by our predecessors and bequeathed by them to us. It includes a full set of religious, moral and cosmological ideas. Nobody is really born naked. Everyone is born into a rich cultural world. Still, every detail of that cultural world, including all its moral and religious ideas, is a product of human art evolved to help us live. It is contingent; it could have been different. It is *baseless*. It can have an art-truth and it can have a pragmatic truth, but it cannot have the old objective sort of Truth-truth. You may think, as I do, that in the affairs of life art-truth and pragmatic truth (plus a spot of logical-consistency-truth) are enough to be going on with. But many people feel that the loss of the old objective sort of Truth plunges them into the Abyss. That is nihilism.

So there is a widespread presumption that the death of God unavoidably leads to the dissolution of the pre-established cosmic order, the collapse of moral values and of the meaningfulness of life, and so to nihilism. But formerly all was well, when God upheld the reality of the world and the moral order. That being so, the best way to conquer nihilism would be to restore the old sort of metaphysical belief in God and the old cosmological and moral realism.

I am going to rock the boat, by casting doubt on this argument. My starting point is a curious and important aesthetic discovery made in recent years by painters and sculptors. It is that realism – by which I mean a programme of attempting perfect, impersonal accuracy in representing something independent of oneself – when pressed to its logical conclusion *itself* topples unexpectedly into nihilism.

A brief introduction to the paradoxes of realism is needed here. Realists see truth as a two-term relationship in which the thing-in-representation is supposed to be a good copy, reproduction, model, imitation, map or whatever of the original-thing-out-there. Thus people like to think that a thought, a belief, a map, a portrait, a sentence or whatever is true if it is life-like, adequate to the original, and an accurate replica, like a tracing. A paradox arises, however, if we ask what happens in the case of a perfect copy. A one-mile-to-the-mile three-dimensional map of Cambridge that exactly reproduced all the detail of Cambridge would in effect *be* Cambridge, and cease to be a *map* at all. By the same reasoning, when the copy gets to be a truly exact replica the status of the original is also threatened, because we can no longer tell which of them is which, or which of them has precedence. So the copying-ideal of truth if pressed hard enough may defeat itself by undermining both the copy and the original.

In our own century the paradoxes of replication have become pervasive. We are capable of ever-more-high-fidelity reproduction of sound, pictures and shapes. The sound on the compact disc you buy has been assembled from the best bits of many performances and then in various ways processed, enhanced and supplemented by engineers. What you hear is something far better than you could ever hear from the artists in person whose names are on the label. Is it still a recording, and if so, of *what*? Or should we regard it as occupying a new realm of hyperreality?

Again, in our time the media representation of the human world is interwoven with our life, part of it and rebounding back upon it. Major crimes like hijacks and sieges that get reported by the media as they occur seem to be conforming themselves to a scenario or archetypal pattern prescribed by the media, so that all concerned are acting out a media script. It is almost as if, by the logic of supplementarity, the media reporting of the event is causing the event to occur. Something similar happens with strikes, football riots, demonstrations, international meetings and much other political action. The event and the representation of it become interwoven, blurred and finally indistinguishable – especially so far as their causation and their effects are concerned.[35]

Games, simulations, media-assisted bluff and enhanced reproductions that are 'better' than the originals are all widespread enough nowadays to be very disorienting to us. In this context consider the implications of the Photo Realist or Super Realist painting that flourished especially in the USA in the 1970s.[36] It grew out of Pop Art, and one can see why. The Renaissance tradition from the fourteenth to the early nineteenth centuries had sought truth to nature, sometimes going into excess and exploring illusionism and *trompe l'oeil* effects. Many members of the public appear to want art to copy nature. The possibility of very accurate reproduction of sound and pictures is a notable technical fact of our time, extensively drawn upon in commercial art and the media. One strand in modern art has reacted by gravitating towards expressionism and abstraction, thus side-stepping any challenge to the camera at what it can do, and instead exploring and making the most of everything the camera cannot do. But there is also the possibility of a neat reversal whereby the artist turns back, meets the camera's challenge head on and tries to outdo it on its own territory. He or she sets out to make a work more real than reality itself, and thereby upsets our sense of reality.

There is an *aporia* here in the traditional notion of an 'illusionistic' art. When the artist makes something that creates the illusion of reality, the work also makes reality seem to be an illusion.

There is a second aspect of the realism-into-nihilism paradox that should be briefly mentioned at this point. There has long been a strand in modern art which finds repellent the humanist idea of art as self-expression. The idea that the artist has a bigger, more interesting and sensitive ego than the rest of us, and has the task of vomiting out a stream of objectifications of it for the rest of us to admire, can indeed seem unappealing. It encourages artists to be big babies and sacred monsters. Why should not art instead seek austerity, discipline, and the disappearance of the individual self? Such an art, undistorted by the claims of the finite greedy ego, would seek a fully detached, objective, calm and world-centred standpoint, seeing the real as it really is.

Unfortunately there is a shocking outcome, for we learn that it is no longer given to us humans to work our way back to a perspectiveless, objective God's-eye-view of the real. When we try to escape our finite human perspectival vision of things we don't gain reality but lose it. Remember Andy Warhol, who thought he was a figment? Warhol's self-denial did not lead him to Reality: on the contrary, the world became *also* a figment, a dance of secondary images. Although he was a Catholic, Warhol could not get back to fifteenth-century realism. Far from it. It seems that such 'reality' as we moderns can get hold of depends entirely on our seeing the world only from our own finite viewpoints, in terms of our own needs and interests, and injecting into it our own partialities and sympathies. For us there can be only a subjective and human realism. When we try to be purely objective and impersonal, the world out there becomes a very thin skin of appearances, as depthless and illusory as the colours in a film of oil on the surface of standing water. In short, it becomes a Super Realist painting.

The Super Realists tried hard for objectivity. They used slide projectors or greatly-enlarged colour photographs. They tried covering every part of the canvas except the area they were currently working on so that in the finished work every bit of the picture, having received just the same close-up attention, would have the same visual weight. The painting would thus be impartial and emotionally perspectiveless. Naturally they liked to use American images: store fronts, diners, autos, bikes. The United States is the most cinematic of all countries. When we are there we seem to ourselves to be in a film. It is the land in which the photographic image seems to precede reality, and to control reality.

The outcome, in the work of such figures as Chuck Close, Duane Hanson, John De Andrea, and Ralph Goings, is well described by the critic Gerrit Henry:

> In Photo Realism, reality is made to look so overpoweringly real as to make it pure illusion: through the basically magical means of point-for-point precisionist rendering the actual is portrayed as being so real that it doesn't exist.[37]

The effect is particularly disturbing in the case of the nude human figure. What you see is not quite a shop-window dummy, which never purports to be anything but a clothes horse; but nor is it like an artist's model posing, nor a body anaesthetized in an operating theatre, nor a corpse. What you see is only a surface. Nothing is withheld and everything is on view, exposed to the point of transparency. Because nothing whatever is held back or in reserve, there is no enquiry to make, no test to carry out, no guessing to do – and this extreme banality has a stupefying effect on the spectator.

The paradox is that *everything is revealed – and so there is nothing there*. Baudrillard calls this 'obscenity'. The technique of expression is so overwhelmingly efficient that what we are presented with has everything up front and nothing at all behind it. We *goggle* in 'the ecstasy of communication', our minds numbed or blown by visual rawness and over-explicitness.

When everything is revealed, there is nothing there. So the ideas of pure revelation and objective reality are empty, just as complete corpse-like exposure is no longer erotic. The real for us human beings is indeed close to the erotic, in that for there to be any 'reality' we must be enticed. Our interest has to be aroused by something still concealed, ambiguous, questionable, teasing, duplicitous, provocative, puzzling and tempting. The problem with Super Realist art is that its only interesting feature is the way it so completely *fails* to interest us. We need an explanation of why a Super Realist nude sculpture which exactly replicates the appearance of a real body is so stupefyingly dull, whereas (for example) Rembrandt's images of Saskia and Hendrickje are so warm and real and unforgettable. When that question is answered, Super Realist art is over (although it is only fair to add that Duane Hanson in particular has made effective use of it as a form of Social Realism).

By draining the world out there of the human feeling we normally project out into it, the Super Realists made the world seem to be just the thinnest of skins. They thus showed that Reality normally gets all its reality *from us*, and in particular from our emotions and our trickery. It is idle to look elsewhere for any other source of reality. Maybe there was such a Source once, but now it has dried up.

The conclusion we draw from all this is that we need to humanize and relativize our ideas of revelation and of objective reality. Purely objective extrahuman reality is a non-entity. It should be replaced by what we may call subjective or human realism. Our sense of reality, as the theatre shows us so well, depends upon emotional involvement, stage effects, provocations and puzzles. Absolute revelation nullifies: as Heidegger's analyses of truth as unconcealment suggested, revelation is always relative to something else that remains hidden, and it must be historically contextualized.[38] Revelation is not and cannot be an absolute thing. It depends on a certain technical and theatrical skill, a feeling for the current mood and a sense of occasion.

A further conclusion I draw is that the traditional conceptions of an objective divine Revelation and of an objective divinely-constituted Reality of things are very problematic. If they meant something and we lost them, well, maybe the loss was not such a serious matter as it seemed at first. Other and more satisfactory conceptions expand to fill their place and do their job better.

Just for example, did God in fact create reality any better than we can? Because his Reality was infinite and that of creatures only finite, there was an annihilating infinite qualitative difference of reality between him and the creature. In preaching, this theme was invoked in order to subvert rather than to strengthen people's sense of reality. Being a creature who has to do with God was compared with treading along a very narrow ledge with an infinite drop on your left and a vast sheer cliff on your right. You teetered along a knife-edge between absolute reality and absolute nothingness. In their different ways the void on your left and the wall of Rock on your right were about equally intimidating. So it is simply not the case that when the old God was around we all felt comfortable and secure with the world firmly set upon its foundations. To take up another of the classic metaphors, like a ping-pong ball bobbing on top of a fountain-jet of water you were held in being from moment to moment by a continual exertion of the divine will. But God had more than enough reason to be highly displeased with you, and at any moment he might turn off the tap. Are there any human beings still alive who remember what serious religion was like? The whole point about the reality of God was *not* that it made you really secure, but that it gave you a real fright. God's reality was annihilating at least as much as it was creative. For most of the Christian era God was seen as having announced the speedy and comprehensive redevelopment of the whole created order. The world suffered from acute planning blight. It was a twilight zone. No very-large-scale project was worth undertaking.

So it is entirely arguable that our modest, projective and libidinally-driven 'human realism' creates a friendlier and more habitable world than we were given by the old objective theologically-based realism.

An analogous case can be made out in connection with the

concept of revelation. God's revelation was never a revelation of absolute theoretical knowledge. It was a revelation of his will and of practical, saving truths. He had revealed a path to salvation and a divine order for human life. The emphasis was upon the adequacy and indeed the finality of a certain way to salvation, with much stress on the concepts of power, authority, command-ments and obedience. From the classical Christian point of view this was moral realism or objectivism, and therefore a Good Thing. God had antecedently created all of moral reality. He had filled all of moral space. You just fitted into, conformed yourself to and obeyed the divinely-ordained moral world-order. You kept the rules, like a good soldier: as the sergeant-major used to shout at us, 'This is the Army; you're not paid to think!' But I now want to say that what used to be described as subjectivism, emotivism or moral anti-realism, and was feared and deplored as anarchic, is much to be preferred. The curse of our century is a kind of nihilistic authoritarianism. We must be pretty desperate if we can think of nothing better to pit a Christian version of it against Stalin's version and Hitler's. Radical Christians, being activists, are moral anti-realists and libertarians. We have to be moral anti-realists, because we have got to imagine that there is scope for us human beings to develop new values and to innovate in morality. We see the Christian life as an historical struggle to actualize Christian values. But nobody can dictate to us in advance exactly what values are to be actualized and how. Historical change is not predictable in advance, and one can no more forecast the future of morality than that of anything else. We've got to have the freedom to respond creatively to the imperative of the moment. And this means that the extent to which past rulings and revelations can prejudge matters is minimal.

In the old Christianity there was, or was thought to be, a pre-established divine reality and divine law. So there was an all-round ready-made world to live in. In the newer account, faith is productive. The Christian tradition is seen as human. We seek to extend it. We have to keep on improvising and amending the reality we live in and the values we live by. Religion becomes less a matter of dogma, authority and obedience, and more a matter of wisdom, insight, creativity and day-to-day *care* for things. We should be poets and curates. The best way to conquer nihilism would be to replace a church that sees its job as guarding the past with one that is confident it can create the future.

(e) Proposals

Although they may walk together for many miles, liberal and radical Christians will eventually find their paths diverging sharply. So long as they limit themselves to discussing the faults of the conservatives, they can find much to agree about. Yes indeed, the conservatives are intellectual authoritarians, anti-humanists, and too dualistic in outlook. Yes, the conservatives are understandably but quite unreasonably suspicious of science and critical thinking. And yes, conservatives are too fetishistic about their dogmas, too factional and intolerant. It takes quite a while to exhaust these very congenial topics, but when they *are* exhausted differences begin to appear. Soon the radicals realize that the liberals are at heart even more conservative, in that they are more content with the cosmic *status quo*, than are the conservatives themselves.

A good indication of this is the way every liberal you ever heard of wants to see less emphasis on spectacular divine interventions to put the world to rights, and more quiet daily satisfaction with the benignity of God's general Providence. Liberals are culture-Christians and cosmic optimists. They believe in continuous, convergent and progressive historical development. They don't care for orthodox Augustinian dualism because as they see it all those contrasting principles (Nature and Grace, the City of Man and the City of God, culture and revelation, etc.) are going to be harmonized, reconciled and unified. The cosmic process is basically friendly, and history is on the side of the angels. Everything is going to come out right in the end. Truth and goodness will prevail. We can relax.

The liberal theology is a developmental theology of creation. Everything ultimately comes together in the 'one far-off divine event/To which the whole creation moves'. Reason and faith, the state and the church are all converging upon a single Goal. It is in keeping with this that the English Modernists of the early twentieth century were often members of the academic establishment, nationalistic in outlook, and Prayer Book conservatives with no very urgent proposals for the structural reform of the church. The Modernists could indeed afford to take their time, if the whole cosmic order of things was on their side. They need not be too aggressive about trying to convert their critics. It was sufficient merely to secure interim toleration for themselves. They wanted their own sweetly reasonable latitudinarian theology recognized as a permissible option within the church and a valid strand of the Christian tradition. In the long run it would prevail anyway.

In their philosophy of religion most liberals are semi-realists.[39] They are of course aware that church imagery presents in hymns and psalms a very primitive picture of the universe as a theocracy ruled by an all-powerful Sky-Father. But this does not unduly worry them, because from their point of view it is not wholly mistaken. In picture-language popular belief in God conveys a profound truth. At a deep level the cosmos is personal, in the long run all shall be well. Thus the liberals, at least during their most confident period, felt at home in the world, at home in the church and even at home with God. Their semi-realism about God may appear vague to critics, but it is of vital importance to them and they defend it strenuously. It does a bridging job. It links the primitive language of prayers, psalms and hymns with their own convictions about the cosmos and the course of history, making them feel able to join in worship with a clear conscience.

Radicals have no such alibi. We see clearly that the liberal ideology is mythical and has collapsed. The notion of historical progress is mythical, and the notion that the cosmos is somehow friendly to us is mythical. We do not have purely objective, culturally-neutral knowledge of how things are cosmically. Once you have got into the habit of noticing the way *all* peoples naïvely first project their own values and cultural conceptions upon the cosmos, and then claim that the cosmos backs them up, you can no longer do it for yourself. You see only too clearly that every claim to cosmic backing is just ideological. Which makes the seemingly naïve realism of the language of worship acutely embarrassing to every thinking Christian. We have tried to put forward a non-realistic interpretation of the language, but the church rejects it. The liberals reject it because they need their vague but optimistic version of theological realism. The conservatives reject it, because they need their demanding, moralistic, threatening sort of God to keep themselves in order. But at this point radicals become very troubled, because along with all pastors and therapists they regard that particular realistic God as extremely damaging. The more realistic your God, the more punitive your morality, the more damaged your psychology and the more blinkered your outlook. To radicals, the somewhat Old-Testament, objectified, monarchical Sky-Father idea of God that prevails in Christian worship is very difficult. The optimistic liberal interpretation of him seems to be mythical and to overlook the facts of evil and suffering. The demanding, repressive conservative interpretation of him seems to be at odds with the gospel. It has always been associated with massive inhumanity, social injustice and psychological damage, and seems therefore to radicals to be deeply unchristian. And as the history of ethics shows, our Christian humanitarianism in fact emerged in the West only through the death of the conservative-realist God.

In reply, theologians naturally claim that the *real* God of Christianity is the God of Gregory of Nazianzus, Anselm, Aquinas or whoever. But whatever the merits of this claim, worship still continues to be in the primitive vocabulary, for power reasons perhaps, or to make radicals uncomfortable; and there is no short-term prospect of reform.

Unlike liberals then, radicals will need to see major changes if they are ever to become really at ease in the church. In the short term we'll have to survive as best we can in the church as it is, by interpreting in a non-realist (that is, symbolic and action-guiding) way all the material that the liberals interpret in a semi-realist way. But this is only a short-term survival strategy, which involves our tolerating too much continuing illusion, untruth and psychological damage to people. In the medium term – perhaps a few generations ahead – we may imagine a Reformed faith.

There are two constraints on the sketch of a Reformed faith that I shall draw. First, it needs to be something that might evolve out of present structures. Secondly, I am still thinking of the church as a people, a *laos* which is manifested in local congregations that meet weekly. Some may think this unrealistic, the argument being that the great majority of people are becoming lumpenconsumers whose lives consist of nothing but work, consumption and the media. Turning out for meetings, and indeed any sort of constructive engagement with society, is not in future to be expected from more than a minute group of professional activists.

I do not think the church can surrender to this view. If she is to be the nursery of new lifestyles and the pioneer of a new order of human relationships, then the church must meet. If it is the case that media hyperreality (including packaging, brand images, stereotypes, stock scenarios, personalities, fashions and fantasies) now constitutes a new World of Forms which completely dominates the culture, then the church may need to develop new methods of 'media-fasting' to liberate people. There is certainly a danger today that ordinary people may altogether lose touch with religion and politics as human practices that they themselves engage in. Instead, religion and politics are becoming just media spectacles – things we watch others do for us.

That said, however, the future church we envisage will be rather different from the present-day church. According to the widely-quoted Lambeth Quadrilateral of 1884 (as reiterated and slightly supplemented in 1920) there will be four criteria of a future united church, and by a happy chance the episcopally-governed churches already satisfy them all. Hence it will be enough in future for us to hold on to what we have already got:

VI. We believe that the visible unity of the Church will be found to involve the whole-hearted acceptance of:

The Holy Scriptures as the record of God's revelation of Himself to man, and as being the rule and ultimate standard of faith; and the Creed commonly called Nicene, as the sufficient statement of the Christian faith, and either it or the Apostles' Creed as the Baptismal confession of belief.

The divinely instituted sacraments of Baptism and the Holy Communion, as expressing for all the corporate life of the whole fellowship, in and with Christ.

A ministry acknowledged as every part of the Church as possessing not only the inward call of the Spirit but also the commission of Christ and the authority of the whole body.

VII. May we not reasonably claim that the Episcopate is the one means of providing such a ministry?[40]

This statement reflects the historic preoccupations with legitimacy, orthodoxy and government, and it is already hopelessly unrealistic. To take just the first criterion, 'the Holy Scriptures': in the most advanced societies the age of the Book is already over.

There is nobody who really gets all her or his guidance for life from the daily study of an ancient and highly complex literary work. Not even the most ardent fundamentalists can make their people do it. Indeed, fundamentalists are notoriously quite as ignorant of the Bible as everybody else. The old skill of living by the Book can no longer exist as it did until the nineteenth century, because the culture has changed. People get their guidance from consulting various technical experts and instruction manuals, and their entertainment from screens. They do not have the extremely delicate and complex literary sensibility that people had in the past. The culture now depends on technique rather than on rhetoric, and as a result the Bible cannot regain its former position. Nor, for rather similar reasons, can the Nicene Creed.

Sacraments, though, there will be. The church will exist in two states, gathered and dispersed. Gathered and become visible, the church will coincide with Christ. Dispersed and invisible, she will coincide with humanity at large. The church's gatherings will take place perhaps at noon on Sundays, or – in some cities – on Thursdays at the end of the working day. The historic buildings will still be in use. The gathering will consist of a common meal, taken seated at table. Each congregation's elected officers will be a group of deacons. One of them will open the meal by standing, banging for attention, and breaking a bread roll, saying: 'the body of Christ', a formula understood to mean that the church now gathered in company is the risen Christ. Noise then breaks out. The meal is simple, like a War on Want lunch. Baskets of fresh bread rolls, cheese, tomatoes, apples. During the meal church business is transacted, items being introduced by the secretaries of the various divisions. Tasks are allocated. The general understanding is that each enrolled member of the church should attend the Meal weekly, and each week should undertake some small task as his or her personal 'liturgy', or item of service. The rhythm is that week by week there is systole and diastole; you come in and you are sent out.

The chief divisions are Study (courses, evening classes, groups), Training (personal counselling, meditation, yoga), Art (music, drama, the visual arts) and Social Action (including local branches of human rights groups, twinning relationships with overseas congregations, and political action). The deacons administer the church, and represent it at the local Synod. It is at

Synod level that the only religious professionals are appointed. They may be designated 'presbyters', and each must have some specialist qualification in theology, psychotherapy, art, drama, social administration or whatever. The local Synod appoints a small group of such people to serve its local congregations. Thus the presbyters function as specialist resource-people for the divisions, but there will be no career religious leaders with spiritual power and sacramental rank. There will be no rulers and no shepherds. All will be priests to each and each to all.

When the business is complete a presbyter, if present, may read a passage from the Gospels and talk about it. There may be some music, or some silence. Then glasses of wine are circulated. A deacon stands and says 'The blood of Christ'. This formula is taken to mean that the church must surrender her distinct identity and must dissolve herself into the common life of humanity. All drink, and the Meeting is over. It has lasted about an hour. If food remains and there are needy people to whom it can be given, then it is given to them, as it was in former times.

Meetings are open to all. Those who wish to join the church as registered members can do so only on Easter Day. They enter at meeting time, wash their own faces in the old Font, sign a register and shake the hand of a member, who receives them with the formula 'In the name of Jesus'. At the Meeting that follows the church's audited annual accounts are approved, and new deacons are elected to serve for the coming year.

The title 'bishop' is given to a respected retired person, not more than one in each local Synod group. The post is honorary, but the person in question is invited to visit local congregations regularly. She or he will be routinely offered the chair at meetings at which she is present, and will be invited to receive new members.

All human groups tend to pressurize their own members, developing a strange conspiracy of reciprocal moral coercion. The church will be much concerned with preventing its own routinization and keeping itself noisy, plural and innovative. Local Synods will appoint a steady stream of young musicians and artists-in-residence. The Art division's task is to find ways of encouraging members of the church to develop their creativity, and the Social Action division will keep looking for new initiatives. Linking meditation, art and social action, the church will strive resolutely to be a society whose only orthodoxy is heresy. Art has to keep on transforming itself; it lives by innovation. Similarly in the church practical proposals of any kind will be assessed by their imaginative merit as innovations, rather than by their conformity to any established norms.

The church will see her mission as the *continuous* reinvention and renewal of humanity. She will be committed to the struggle for social justice and liberty, and to philanthropic action. But since 'humanity' has no fixed essence, the church has to keep on reinventing it. No earlier political theory was able to recognize this need. The church must therefore combine the discipline and good order required for effective corporate action with the extreme libertarianism of a society which, like an art school, must foster creativity and individuality. Through inability to reconcile these conflicting demands revolutionary groups have so far either succeeded, only to create fresh tyrannies, or failed, and petered out. Our suggestion is that the church should have and value a framework of good order, but the bars must be as thin as possible. The only non-oppressive discipline is scepticism, minimalism, emptiness, the discipline of the Void. So we are likely to need something like Buddhist meditation for individuals, and in corporate life extreme doctrinal reticence, simplicity and a consistent policy of encouraging difference, freedom and innovation.

Should we not already be working towards something of this sort? It will certainly not be possible, or even desirable, abruptly to abolish the old beliefs and observances and to replace them with the new. But the new might begin to grow alongside or within the shell of the old. The new order might appear in a religious society, or in the student world. Then as the old order fades away the new one may gradually expand to fill the resulting vacuum.

Remember that we have described only a very thin framework, within which there is space for people to experiment with many different spiritualities, beliefs and moralities. Many will continue to be theists. They will explore their personal visions of God and they will pray to their personal gods. For reasons to do with the dangers of too great a concentration of power, the church will not have a centred, common God, but there may well be dispersed, personalized divinity. In general the design-requirement for a future church is *not* to create a new pattern, but to open a space for plurality, for humanity and for spiritual freedom.

Such a church, structurally democratic, credally minimalist and consistently libertarian, will be the first genuinely radical Christian church, and perhaps the sort of church for which Latin American Christianity is currently groping.[41] For strategic reasons it is not possible for the theology of liberation to become intellectually explicit as yet. Given the nature of the Roman Catholic system, it would be most unwise to embark upon the intellectual argument before the moral argument has been irreversibly won. So Liberation Theology uses traditional super-naturalist terminology in a cloudy and metaphorical way, and avoids spelling out the precise philosophical status of its God-talk. For the present, perhaps, it has to be so.

However, in the long run we will need to become more honest. We have to admit that there is a world of difference between those who think we should pray and wait passively for God to put the world to rights, and those who think it is now up to us. In the long run you cannot struggle for open civil democracy on earth while believing that a mysterious absolute monarchy prevails and must continue to prevail in heaven and in the church.

Thus it is imperative that the radical Christian struggle for social justice be accompanied by the reform and modernization of the church and her beliefs. Maybe this cannot be done yet in Latin America; but it must be done soon, or all the efforts of Christians will merely prove self-defeating. As for us in the West, there are many who say that we need our own version of Liberation Theology, and there are now many who are sincerely committed to struggling as Christians for social justice, peace and human rights. We will the end, so is it not time that we willed the means?

Notes

Introduction

1. For the account of Freud's views that follows, see especially *Totem and Taboo* (1912) and *Group Psychology and the Analysis of the Ego* (1921).

1. *The Trouble with Believing*

1. On the importance of avoiding misunderstanding on this point see Richard Harland, *Superstructuralism: The Philosophy of Structuralism and Post-Structuralism*, Methuen 1987, pp. 167f.

2. Paul Feyerabend, *Against Method: Outline of an Anarchistic Theory of Knowledge*, London: Verso Editions 1978. Many philosophers less thoroughgoing than Feyerabend speak instead of 'overcoming epistemology', i.e. scrapping any disciplinary controls or censorship of the process of knowledge-production. 'Overcoming epistemology' in philosophy equals 'overcoming orthodoxy' in theology. We don't need a policeman.

3. Gilles Deleuze and Felix Guattari, *Anti-Oedipus*, 1972; ET, London: the Athlone Press 1984.

4. Mark C. Taylor, *Altarity*, Chicago 1987, hints at the possibility of a form of religious thought that rejoices in difference.

2. *We are Grateful to Art*

1. Schopenhauer is a good example of a philosopher whose view of art remains – quite inconsistently, as one might well think – Platonic and spectatorial or contemplative.

2. Especially in 'Violence and Metaphysics: An Essay on the Thought of Emmanuel Levinas'; in Jacques Derrida, *Writing and Difference*, 1967; ET, Routledge & Kegan Paul 1978, ch. 4.

3. For the material in this paragraph, see Bernard Williams, *Ethics and the Limits of Philosophy*, Collins Fontana 1985, pp. 32f.

4. *Principles of Church Reform*, 1833.

3. *The Only Christianity that we can Believe Now* ...

1. David Pears (ed.), *Russell's Logical Atomism*, Collins Fontana 1972, p. 52.

2. Friedrich Nietzsche, *Human, All Too Human*, One: 2; trans. University of Nebraska Press 1984, pp. 14f.

3. W. K. C. Guthrie comments on this: *A History of Greek Philosophy*, Vol. IV, Cambridge 1975, p. 506 and n. 2. Other things said here are a reconsideration and a revision of my earlier assessment of feminism in *Crisis of Moral Authority* 1972, ²1985, ch. 3.

4. On the sacredness of semen, e.g. Mary Douglas, *Purity and Danger*, 1966; Ark edition 1984, pp. 126f. For the themes under discussion here see also her *Natural Symbols*, Barrie & Rockliff 1970.

5. For much more detail, see Fatna A. Sabbah, *Woman in the Muslim Unconscious*, Pergamon 1984, a devastating indictment.

6. Nietzsche is often thought of as a very masculine writer. Derrida draws attention to an opposite undercurrent in him, which surfaces in 'Truth is a Woman': *Spurs/Eperons*, University of Chicago 1978.

7. Bonhoeffer, Letter to E. Bethge of 16 July 1944. See *Letters and Papers from Prison*, The Enlarged Edition, SCM Press 1971, pp. 357ff.

8. Sabbah, cited above, n. 5, is particularly illuminating on all this.

9. See the useful remarks of Nelson Garver, in his Preface to Jacques Derrida, *Speech and Phenomena*, Evanston: North Western University 1973.

10. Here I am indebted to the writings of Wilfred Cantwell Smith, especially *The Meaning and End of Religion*, Macmillan 1963.

11. A thesis explored in George A. Lindbeck, *The Nature of Doctrine: Religion and Theology in a Postliberal Age*, SPCK 1984.

12. I here invoke standard post-structuralist doctrine about language. See, for example, Jean-Jacques Lecercle, *Philosophy through the Looking-Glass: Language, nonsense, desire*, Hutchinson 1985.

13. Using the word 'scientific' here in the old metaphysical and *pre-scientific* sense.

14. Ignatius, *To the Ephesians*, 6. On the Divine Silence, see for example Pseudo-Dionysius, *Mystical Theology*, 1; *Divine Names* 4, 22 (C. E. Rolt translations, SPCK 1951, pp. 191, 119). On Christ as the Word proceeding from God's Silence, see Ignatius, *To the Magnesians*, 8.

15. Ignatius, *To the Ephesians*, 15: 'It is better to keep silence and to be, than to talk and not to be' (J. B. Lightfoot translation). You make yourself more of a substance by shutting up. Because, archaically, men think women a bit less substantial than men, they assume women must talk too much. So male writers commend silence in women: I Clement 22, etc., etc.

16. There has been very sharp controversy about this matter. See, for example, Edmund Leach, 'Virgin Birth', *Proceedings of the Royal Anthropological Institute*, 1966, pp. 39–50, attacked by M. E. Spiro, 'Virgin birth, parthenogenesis and physiological paternity: an essay in cultural interpretation', *Man* N.S. III, 1968, pp. 242–261.

4. . . . Is Unacceptable to the Church

1. E.g., *Apostolicam Actuositatem*, Decree of the Second Vatican Council, 18 November 1965.
2. Graham Shaw, *The Cost of Authority*, SCM Press 1983.
3. *The Gay Science*, §358; Walter Kaufmann translation, New York: Vintage Books 1974, p. 313.
4. *Antichrist*, §§29ff.
5. Alasdair MacIntyre, *Whose Justice? Which Rationality?*, Duckworth 1988, p. 10.
6. The literature of postmodernism is now very large indeed. Among works that remain useful are: Allan Megill, *Prophets of Extremity*, University of California Press 1985; Jean-François Lyotard, *The Postmodern Condition*, ET, Manchester University Press 1984; and Hal Foster (ed.), *Postmodern Culture*, London and Sydney: Pluto Press 1983.
7. See my *Life Lines*, SCM Press 1986, ch. 5.
8. Richard Swinburne, *The Coherence of Theism*, 1977; *The Existence of God*, 1979; *Faith and Reason*, 1981; *The Evolution of the Soul*, 1986 (all Oxford: the Clarendon Press).
9. On all this see Jacques Derrida, *Spurs: Nietzsche's Styles*, French-English version, University of Chicago Press 1979.
10. *Critique of Pure Reason*, B xvii f.
11. Best exposition: Emil L. Fackenheim, *The Religious Dimension in Hegel's Thought*, University of Chicago Press, 1982 ed., especially pp. 129–154.
12. W. E. H. Stanner, *On Aboriginal Religion*, Sydney 1963.
13. See for example, Fatna A. Sabah, cited at ch. 3, n. 5 above.
14. I mention Judah by way of tribute to my late friend Rabbi Sholem Singer of Highland Park, Illinois, who translated and edited him in a work entitled *Medieval Jewish Mysticism*. At the time of writing I am unable to trace a copy.
15. *The Sentences of Pseudo-Phocylides*, 11.213f. Hellenistic influence, surely? There are in fact other references, such as II Enoch 10.4 (J), which remind us, if reminder were needed, that the dark side of male sexuality is not a recent cultural formation.
16. My distinguished colleague Peter Burke thinks I am wrong to push 'period' back as far as Flacius. For a more sober account see Reinhart Koselleck, *Futures Past: On the Semantics of Historical Time*, trans. Keith Tribe, MIT Press 1985; pp. 246f.

17. I have taken a hint in these last few paragraphs from Jean Baudrillard, 'The year 2000 Will Not Take Place', in *Futur* Fall: Excursions into Post-Modernity*, ed. E. A. Grosz, Terry Threadgold and others (Power Institute Publications 4), Sydney 1986. But Baudrillard is on the whole pessimistic about the end of history, whereas I take it that a Christian should be optimistic. Life is indeed objectively aimless, but through the practice of our religion we *can* develop the strength to recreate meaning and values. The modern Christian must preach the possibility of redesigning the world. We follow Foucault, not Freud. Nature is not a fixed limit: it can be refashioned.

5. Strategies for Christian Survival

1. Etienne Gilson, *God and Philosophy*, Yale University Press 1941.
2. See Robin Horton, 'African Traditional Thought and Western Science', in Bryan R. Wilson (ed.), *Rationality*, Oxford: Blackwell 1977, pp. 131–171; esp. pp. 162ff. Horton thinks that both traditional religion and modern science postulate hidden entities to explain events, but because religious entities are powerful, well-informed and personal it is highly imprudent to criticize them directly. They have limitless power to punish you for your presumption. Thus religious beliefs so-to-say protect themselves from falsification. Instead of giving up faith, I judge it safer to resort to what Evans-Pritchard called 'secondary elaboration'. I make excuses for God, saying for example that he must have had his own good reasons, unknown to us, for allowing a disaster to occur, or for not answering our prayers.
3. See Robert Browning's poem, 'Bishop Bloughram's Apology'.
4. For example, in a 1968 debate with John A. T. Robinson, Bernard Williams suggested that certain beliefs 'must be held if it is Christianity that is being believed at all', and one of them is that 'God is transcendent to human affairs and to human attitudes . . . even if there were no human beings or human aspirations, there would still be a God.' Theological realism is of the essence, Williams claims. See Bernard Williams and John A. T. Robinson, 'Has "God" a Meaning? – A Discussion', *Question* No. 1 (1968), last reprinted in Paul Edwards and Arthur Pap, *A Modern Introduction to Philosophy*, Macmillan, New York: The Free Press, 1973, pp. 534–544. My quotations from pp. 537f.
5. *Appearance and Reality*, Chapters XXV, XXVI; *Essays on Truth and Reality*, Chapter XV. The precise wording I use is derived from the *Essays*, first edition, Oxford 1914, p. 428.
6. *Culture and Value*, translated by Peter Winch, Oxford: Blackwell 1980, pp. 50e, 53e, 64e, 82e.
7. See for example, Anthony Storr, *Jung*, Collins Fontana 1973, ch. 6, and the passages from Jung there cited.
8. See his *Letters and Papers from Prison*, The Enlarged Edition, SCM Press 1971.

9. E.g., *Concluding Unscientific Postscript*, tr. D. F. Swenson and Walter Lowrie, Princeton University Press 1941, p. 540.

10. Rush Rhees (ed.) *Ludwig Wittgenstein: Personal Recollections*, Oxford: Blackwell 1981, p. 129.

11. From 'Only a God Can Save Us: Der Speigel's Interview with Martin Heidegger', *Philosophy Today*, 20 (1976), p. 277; cited in Allan Megill, *Prophets of Extremity*, University of California Press 1985, p. 136.

12. For a useful review of Murdoch on the religious life, try Elizabeth Dipple, *Iris Murdoch: Work for the Spirit*, Methuen 1982.

13. Rush Rhees, as cited above, n. 10, ibid.

14. A point well made by Ernest Gellner: *Legitimation of Belief*, Cambridge University Press 1974, especially ch. 9.

15. Some details in, for example, A. M. G. Stephenson, *The Rise and Decline of English Modernism*, SPCK 1984; Keith W. Clements, *Lovers of Discord: Twentieth Century Theological Controversies in England*, SPCK 1988.

16. II Corinthians 6.8.

17. See, in particular, ps.-Dionysius, *The Ecclesiastical Hierarchy* and *The Angelic Hierarchy*.

6. What is to be Done?

1. T. J. J. Altizer, 'Theology as Reflection upon the Roots of Christian Culture'; in Theodore W. Jennings Jr (ed.), *The Vocation of the Theologian*, Philadelphia: Fortress Press 1985, pp. 138ff.

2. See my *The Long-Legged Fly*, 1987, and *The New Christian Ethics*, 1988.

3. For philosophical reflections on the media age, see especially the work of Jean Baudrillard.

4. Battling with this problem – from a markedly conservative standpoint – is Alasdair MacIntyre, *Whose Justice? Which Rationality?*, Duckworth 1988.

5. E.g., Council of Nicea, Canon 17; Apostolic Canons, 44.

6. Jean Milet, *God or Christ?*, tr. John Bowden, SCM Press 1981. I agree in the main with Milet's timetable but not his analysis.

7. D. Z. Phillips, *The Concept of Prayer*, Oxford: Blackwell 1965, ²1981.

8. Graham Shaw, *God in Our Hands*, SCM Press 1987, passim.

9. Edward Craig, *The Mind of God and the Works of Man*, Cambridge University Press 1987, pp. 271, 290.

10. Keiji Nishitani, *Religion and Nothingness*, University of California Press 1982.

11. Sören Kierkegaard, *Philosophical Fragments* (Swenson translation, revised and edited by Howard V. Hong) Princeton 1962, pp. 92f. I was prompted to re-read the 'Interlude' in the *Fragments* by Frederick

Sontag. It is a remarkable piece of writing, and doubtless open to widely different interpretations.

12. Ibid., p. 96.
13. Ibid., amended.
14. Ibid., p. 93.
15. Ibid., p. 99.
16. Ibid., p. 100.
17. Ibid., p. 101.
18. Ibid.
19. Ibid., p. 55.
20. Ibid., pp. 105, 104, 103.
21. Ibid., p. 108.
22. Ibid.
23. *Concluding Unscientific Postscript*, Princeton 1941 ed., p. 540.
24. A point well made by Julian Roberts, in a good short discussion of the messianic philosophy of history: *German Philosophy: An Introduction*, Oxford: The Polity Press 1988, pp. 5–8.
25. Galatians 3.24.
26. See the text referred to in ch. 4, note 17, above.
27. In the journal *Encounter* especially.
28. I am here misusing the title of J.-F. Lyotard, *Economie Libidinale*, Paris: Minuit 1974.
29. On all this, see Baudrillard's later writings, for example *In the Shadow of the Silent Majorities . . .*, *Simulations*, *Forget Foucault/Forget Baudrillard*, and *The Ecstasy of Communication*, all published New York, Columbia University: Semiotext (e) 1983, 1983, 1987, 1988; and *The Evil Demon of Images*, Sydney: Power Institute Publications no. 3, 1987. Mark Poster has edited *Jean Baudrillard: Selected Writings*, Polity Press 1988. See also Douglas Kellner, *Jean Baudrillard: From Marxism to Post-Modernism and Beyond*, Polity Press 1989.
30. E.g., J.-F. Lyotard, *The Postmodern Condition*, Manchester University Press 1984. And see Geoffrey Bennington, *Lyotard: Writing the Event*, Manchester University Press 1988.
31. E.g., Brian Easlea, *Witch-Hunting, Magic and the New Philosophy*, Sussex: Harvester Press 1980.
32. *Timaeus* 50D.
33. At different stages in his career, and in different works, Heidegger gave various slightly different accounts of just what the supposed philosophical Fall had consisted in. My short summary is close to what he says in the second volume of his book on Nietzsche.
34. *The New Christian Ethics*, SCM Press 1988.
35. On all this, see especially Baudrillard's *Simulations* and *The Ecstasy of Communication*, referred to above.
36. Edward Lucie-Smith, *Super Realism*, Oxford: Phaidon Press 1979.

37. Cited by Lucie-Smith, op. cit., p. 7.

38. On Heidegger's philosophy of the history of Being, seeing the interesting discussion by Michael Allen Gillespie, *Hegel, Heidegger, and the Ground of History*, University of Chicago Press 1984, ch. 5.

39. 'Semi-realism': a term I introduced in *Life Lines* (1986). It describes positions like that of Bishop John Robinson.

40. Cited from H. Bettenson, *Documents of the Christian Church*, Oxford University Press 1943, p. 443.

41. On this point, and for views very different from mine, see Christopher Rowland, *Radical Christianity*, Polity Press 1988.

Index of Names

Adorno, T., 146
Altizer, T. T. J., 127, 178
Anselm, 118
Aquinas, Thomas, 168
Aristotle, 102, 134
Arnold, T., 28, 154
Augustine, 65ff., 123

Baudrillard, J., 147, 163, 177ff.
Bauer, B., 67
Bennington, G., 179
Bethge, E., 175
Bettenson, H., 180
Beuys, J., 24
Blake, W., 127
Bogart, H., 150
Bonhoeffer, D., 49, 110, 175
Bowden, J. S., 178
Bradley, F. H., 110
Browning, R., 107, 177
Burke, U. P., 176

Calvin, J., 49, 96
Chomsky, N., 54
Clements, K. W., 178
Close, Chuck, 162
Comte, A., 8
Cosin, J., 149
Craig, E., 141, 178

Dante, 123, 127
Darwin, C., 8, 41
De Andrea, John, 162
Deleuze, G., 16, 174

Derrida, J., 22, 45, 50, 107, 174ff.
Descartes, K., 39, 84, 102, 123, 135
Dipple, E., 178
Dostoyevsky, F., 72, 116
Douglas, M., 175
Drury, C., 116, 121
Durkheim, E., 19, 41
Dworkin, A., 115

Easlea, B., 179
Edwards, P., 177
Einstein, A., 119
Evans-Pritchard, E. E., 177

Fackenheim, E., 176
Feuerbach, L. A., 8, 67
Feyerabend, P., 15, 174
Flacius Illyricus, 98, 176
Foster, H., 176
Foucault, M., 177
Francis of Assisi, 72
Frege, G., 36
Freud, S., 2ff., 8, 41, 52, 114f., 174,
  177

Garver, N., 175
Gellner, E., 178
Gillespie, M. A., 179
Gilson, E., 102, 177
Goings, Ralph, 162
Graves, R., 153
Gregory of Nazianzus, 168
Grosz, E. A., 177
Guattari, F., 174

Guthrie, W. K. C., 175

Hanson, Duane, 162f.
Harland, R., 174
Hawking, S., 119
Hegel, G. W. F., 20, 28, 30f., 40f.,
  77, 83, 88, 114, 117, 124, 135,
  143, 145
Heidegger, M., 41, 77, 120, 146,
  155, 163, 179f.
Hick, J. H., 19
Holderlin, F., 114
Horton, R., 177
Huxley, J. S., 136

Ignatius of Antioch, 61, 175
Innocent III, 72

James, W., 141
Jennings, T. W., Jr., 178
Judah the Pious, 93
Jung, C. G., 104, 110, 177
Justinian, 27

Kant, I., 20, 52, 84f., 124, 135
Kellner, D., 179
Kierkegaard, S., 1, 7, 67, 72, 110,
  115, 143ff., 178
Kosellek, R., 176

Lacan, J., 4
Leach, E. R., 176
Lecerck, J.-J., 175
Leibniz, G. W., 21f.
Lewis, C. S., 140
Lindbeck, G. A., 175
Lowrie, W., 178
Lyndesay, D., 140
Lyotard, J.-F., 176, 179
Luther, M., 72

MacDonald, G., 140
Machen, A., 140
MacIntyre, A. C., 77, 176, 178
Mackie, J. L., 16
Mallarmé, S., 11
Marx, K., 4, 8, 41, 52, 135, 146
Megill, A., 176, 178

Milet, J., 178
Milton, J., 127
Montaigne, F. de, 20
Murdoch, I., 116, 120, 178

Nelson, H., 68f.
Nesbit, E., 140
Neuberger, J., 32f.
Nietzsche, F. W., 4, 11, 19ff., 41ff.,
  50, 72f., 77, 83, 146ff., 158, 175,
  179
Nishitani, K., 178

Pap, A., 177
Pears, D. F., 175
Phillips, D. Z., 178
Pierce, C. S., 11
Plato, 40, 81, 102, 134, 154f.
Poster, M., 179
Ps.-Dionysius, 178

Rembrandt, 163
Rhees, R., 178
Roberts, J., 179
Robinson, J. A. T., 141, 177, 180
Rolt, C. E., 175
Rothko, Mark, 25f.
Rowland, C. C., 180
Russell, B., 35f.

Sabbah, F. A., 175f.
Salome, L., 114
Sartre, J.-P., 114
Schleiermacher, F. D. E., 28, 124
Schopenhauer, A., 174
Shakespeare, W., 14, 21f.
Shaw, G., 72, 176, 178
Singer, S., 176
Smith, W. C., 175
Spinoza, B., 21
Spiro, M. E., 176
Stanner, W. E. H., 176
Stephenson, A. M. G., 178
Storr, A., 177
Strauss, D. F., 178
Swinburne, R. G., 81, 176

Taylor, M. C., 174

Tennyson, A., 8
Threadgold, T., 177
Tielhard de Chardin, P., 136
Tolstoy, L., 72, 116
Tribe, K., 176

Vidal, G., 141
Vivekananda, 19

Warhol, A., 161

Waugh, E., 24
Weil, S., 116
Whitehead, A. N., 136
Williams, B., 24ff., 174, 177
Williams, C., 140
Wilson, B. R., 177
Winch, P., 177
Wittgenstein, L., 35, 50, 110, 116,
    121, 135
Wordsworth, W., 114